Author's Note

This is an interactive book. It has its own blog at www.2010ablueprintforchange.com. This means you can register your own views and comments and see what other bloggers have said. The purpose is to stimulate debate. You may love my ideas or you may hate them. You may have better ones of you own. You may have experiences to share.

To make reference easier the book is divided into seven Parts, six dedicated to a key forum of debate in our country today. The seventh draws some of the threads together. The chapters are kept short and run consecutively through all the Parts.

I hope you enjoy the read. Above all I hope you feel better able to make your own choices about the future of our country and thus the future for us all.

I0038891

For Lara

2010
A Blueprint for Change

Malcolm Blair-Robinson

Published 2009 by arima publishing

www.arimapublishing.com

ISBN 978 1 84549 391 2

Printed and bound in the United Kingdom

Typeset in Garamond 12

arima publishing
ASK House, Northgate Avenue
Bury St Edmunds, Suffolk IP32 6BB
t: (+44) 01284 700321

www.arimapublishing.com

2010
A Blueprint for Change

Contents

PART ONE
The Economy
Chapters 1 - 8

PART TWO
Foreign Affairs
Chapters 9 - 15

PART THREE
The Constitution
Chapters 16 - 24

PART FOUR
Health
Chapters 25 - 30

PART FIVE
Education
Chapters 31 - 37

PART SIX
Quality of Life
Chapters 38 - 44

PART SEVEN
A More Practical State
Chapters 45 – 54

2010
A Blueprint for Change.
Part One
Chapters 1-8

The Economy

This first chapter deals with the issue which is the number one priority for most people. It will concentrate on the structural faults which have brought about the present crisis. As government action at several levels will have been taken and will continue whilst this book is being written and after publication, the narrative will explore options and dangers and endeavour to inject new thinking.

The Global Financial Crisis has its origins in the UK and the US. Both countries made the error of supposing that it was possible to sustain economic prosperity almost entirely on consumer borrowing secured by ever inflating property values, while general inflation remained low. Banks and other financial institutions abandoned all the caution natural to their calling inventing new kinds of assets which nobody understood and took risks on a scale that brought them all to the brink of collapse. The ripple effect produced the global element, but the origins were not global.

The US, with its huge industrial and high tech manufacturing base and its vast natural resources is better placed to engineer its recovery than we are. We have to navigate a very dangerous piece of uncharted sea. The whole economy, consumers especially, is spectacularly over borrowed and the levels of debt are a cause of the strangulation. Most of the banks are over borrowed. There can be no lasting recovery until debt levels are reduced. This should be the focus of every remedy.

On all sides there is clamour for government to intervene. Whatever is done must be focussed on the long term and on restoring the integrity of the financial structure. At all costs we must come out of the crisis riding a different economic model to the one that took us in. We need to accept what few dare to say. The western financial model of which the U.S and the U.K were the principal architects has imploded. Of all the countries affected it is now the widely held view that the U.K. may have the biggest problems.

This is the greatest financial crisis for a century and perhaps since the industrial revolution. It can be managed, but not without fundamental changes in the way our society values the sum of its endeavour and not without pain. If we take the long view and go the whole mile, we will sustain essential the structure of modern life and emerge stronger in the end. This may take a generation.

If we go into denial and think that the route is to borrow our way out of our debts, there will be untold numbers of unemployed, a valueless currency and a daily grimness recalling dark days of the past. The issue will move from being a financial crisis to a government debt crisis. That is the worst crisis of all.

1

I was born shortly before the outbreak of World War II. The economy had emerged from the depression helped by some public works and a great deal of rearmament. After the war the doctrine of John Maynard Keynes was fully embraced by a Labour government trying to engineer major social reform, hampered by the austere condition of the nation which had won the war but broken its financial back in the process.

Those who lived through those post war times will not forget that austerity period, the shortages, the make do and mend. Yet it was a period of hope, of full employment, of improving standards for working people, of an end to what were referred to as the bad old days. Later a confident Conservative Prime Minister told the nation it had never had it so good. The nation agreed and returned him to power at the general election of 1959 with his majority doubled. Soon things turned sour. The economy overheated. A new phrase was coined; *stop-go*.

By 1964 Labour was back, aided somewhat by a juicy sex scandal and the feeling that the Tories with their grouse moor image were out of date. There had been something of an economic recovery and we were in a *go* period. Science and technology, the new Prime Minister promised, would bring its white heat to build Britain anew. But it was not to be. A balance of payments crisis followed by devaluation, a national humiliation in the days of fixed exchange rates, led in 1970 to a Conservative government again. Then came the dash for growth, as it was called at the time. The pound was floated and the fixed exchange rate abandoned. Fiscal policy was relaxed. The economy took off.

Not, unfortunately, in the right direction. Instead of increasing industrial investment and efficiency to catch up on our competitors, the ones who had lost the war but seemed to have won the peace, we entered a property boom. In the City a new kind of animal reigned supreme in the jungle, the asset stripper. In the high street fringe banks popped up. Credit cards became the new way of paying.

Suddenly the Egyptians caught the seemingly omnipotent Israelis by surprise, crossed the Suez Canal and fanned out across the Sinai desert. The Syrians attacked the Golan Heights. All of which might have been resolved as with past conflicts in the area, without much impact on the rest of the world, but for the fact that the Arabs used the oil weapon, which a myopic West had not seen they were

11

holding. Overnight the price of oil, stable since the war, doubled.

The impact on the British economy was calamitous. The fringe banks collapsed. The asset stripping companies went bust. The clever new financial instruments they favoured to finance their expansion were found to be worthless. Inflation moved to double digits and continued to climb. The miners went on strike. The lights went out. The government called a snap election with the theme 'who governs Britain?' Not you, said the people. Labour was back. It did no better.

Rampant trade unions were ceded ever more power. Inflation remained excessive. Taxation became ridiculous. The public finances went into freefall. The IMF had to come and bail the country out. The unions went potty and demanded more and more. The winter of discontent cast its chill across the land. The people had had enough. The Government lost a vote of confidence in the Commons and resigned. A reeling and battered nation turned in desperation to a housewife. Her name was Margaret Thatcher.

There followed the greatest slaughter of sacred cows in the nation's history. Nothing was spared. Union power, full employment, public ownership, high taxation, state regulation and much else took the forlorn path to the abattoir where the lady waited with a glint in her eye and an axe in her hand.

Yet the people loved it. The left moved further left and were routed. Socialism disappeared. Communism, the Soviet type anyway collapsed. These isms, as one minister told an ecstatic Tory conference, had become wasms. There was now only one ism now. Thatcherism.

Thus began, through a partnership with the U.S version known as Reaganomics, the development of a philosophy that said the markets were the dominant factor in the economy, of which the energy was ever increasing consumer spending, fuelled by more and more borrowing, supposedly secured by ever rising house prices, yet without inflation of any significance in the economy generally.

The State busied itself with reforms in education and health which made no difference, and inventing never ending regulations to supervise the new freedoms. Best practice became the mantra. Commonsense was derided and ceased to be a factor of management. The purpose of the citizen was little more than to go shopping. This was all that was needed. The relevance or usefulness of the work undertaken to produce the income to fund the debt payments ceased to be important.

A new terminology was adopted to hide the danger of all this folly. Debt became credit. Borrowing more became equity release. Spending became investment. Boom and bust were declared by Labour, fully converted to the new philosophy and now in power on a landslide, to be at an end. Of course it could not go on. Commonsense could have warned where best practice was blind. Suddenly it was here. The Credit Crunch.

Soon this became the Global Financial Crisis. It has now become the Global Recession. It is in fact the collapse of the free market financial model. Nobody knows what will follow. Like all endings it has its root in its beginnings, yet those who began it did not see it ending this way. Indeed had they still been around they may have stopped it short before harm was done. But we are where we are.

Where are we exactly?

Does anyone know?

Fetch an economist, I hear you say. Yet all my adult life I have been listening to economists saying different things at different times. They never seem to get it right. Mostly they are part right and part wrong.

2

If you are clever or an economist you can skip the next eight paragraphs.

So as to clear the mind let us begin with a question. What is an economy? Most of us lose concentration when clever mathematicians explain. Let us try to get to the root of the matter, by going back to the beginning. Imagine an early human settlement where each family grew its own food, hunted its own meat, built its own hut and drew its own water from a spring. Clothes were made from the skins of the slain beasts and fuel came from wood gathered from the forest. Everyone is self sufficient. There is no economy.

Then one day two neighbours get to talk and one, the better hunter, agrees to hunt for both. In exchange the other promises to grow sufficient for two families, as he is the better grower. Soon these two improve their skills to the point where they can hunt and grow for many families. The economy starts to form.

As they have no need of more harvest or meat in exchange, they hit upon the idea of coloured pebbles, quite rare and from a pit high up the hillside, being used as tokens of exchange. Soon these can be used for buying skins and clothes and then before long everyone in the valley is contributing to some aspect of the needs of life, exchanging their offering for coloured pebbles which they in turn can exchange again. Now they have a currency.

Eventually an elder suggests that rather than plod up and down the valley with their offerings and collecting orders, they meet in one spot, all together, on a fixed day regularly, bringing all their wares ready for exchange for pebbles. This meeting they call the market. Soon there are so many pebbles, now of great value, that a safe place is needed to keep them. A guarded store is built and called a bank. Everyone puts their spare pebbles in this safe place and soon there is a mighty hoard. The chief guard, called the banker, has a very clever idea.

If people from time to time need more pebbles than they actually own, the bank will provide them for a fixed period. Each borrower will make his mark on a parchment to show what he owes. To make it worthwhile the bank will require the return one more pebble in ten for each year the borrower has use of the extra pebbles.

This works well and soon the farmers in the valley are making all kinds of improvements to boost their output and as the numbers of pebbles in circulation grows, more are dug out of the hillside to keep pace with demand. Then one day a traveller from a far valley arrives and says to the banker 'I will lend you even more pebbles in exchange for the pieces of parchment that your borrowers have signed and then you will be able to lend more and more'. The banker jumps at this opportunity. Things then start to go wrong.

Soon many farmers and hunters give up their hard work. Some begin buying and selling the pieces of parchment, which the clever traveller sells to them for pebbles which they have borrowed. There is so much activity that a financial market is set up. Other farmers and hunters begin to buy and sell each others' huts and land, demanding ever more pebbles for each transaction. It is not long before almost nobody does the old work of husbandry as everyone can buy all they need from the produce of other valleys far and wide. They use pebbles mostly borrowed from the banker, who borrows from the traveller. In the end they value the pebbles for their own sake, not for what they represent.

It happens now that fate, ever watchful of human frailty, takes a hand. A storm comes and damages one of the few producing farmer's crops and hut. To pay for the repairs he decides to go to the bank and take out his pebbles. He is the only person in the valley to use his own pebbles and not the borrowed ones. But the banker does not have enough pebbles left. He only has pieces of parchment. The banker appeals to the traveller who is deaf to his frantic cry. Panic breaks out. No one wants parchment. Desperate people try to sell their huts and land but there are not enough pebbles to pay. The pit on the hillside is empty.

There is one burning question. Where are all the pebbles? They are in the far off valleys with the people who produced the goods, so the erstwhile farmers and hunters in our valley could buy and trade in parchments, using borrowed pebbles to pay for their needs.

This is where we return to our modern world, in which the global financial system has suffered its greatest crisis in history. To discover something of what has happened, we first need to find the pebbles, or in modern terms, money expressed in the most powerful currency on earth, the US dollar.

What we find is, for the West, deeply shocking.

America is the world's largest economy and Britain ranks number four. Yet by the measure of foreign currency reserves we rank numbers 22 and 23, each with a little over $70 billion. This compares with $137 billion for Germany and $113 billion for France and $97 billion for Italy. These three countries did not engage in the borrow and spend spree of the last decade with the same level of abandon as we and our U.S friends. But the real fright comes when you find who really holds the cash. China $1.9 trillion, Japan $995billion, Russia $515billion, India $283 billion, Taiwan $281 billion. In fact more than one third of all the world's reserves are held by Chinese nations. Even countries like Poland, Mexico and Turkey are ahead of us in this league.

Although gold is no longer used as the standard by which currency is secured, the US still holds over 8000 tonnes, which represents about 80% of their total reserves, inclusive of foreign currency. Germany is next with 3400 tonnes, then France 2500 tonnes and Italy 2400 tonnes. All these countries hold more foreign exchange than the UK and have more than 50% of their total reserves in gold. In the UK we are way behind in foreign exchange, but we have only a mere 300 tonnes of gold, which is only 14% of our total reserves.

The most alarming figures are the numbers relating to overseas debt. This is the total figure each country owes to foreign countries because of borrowing abroad. It excludes money owed to ourselves internally. Unsurprisingly America, coming down from a borrowing binge and with the largest economy, tops the list at $£13.7 trillion. This is just equal to its GDP. The UK comes next in line with a total of $10.45 trillion. This is a staggering 3.5 times our GDP or nearly $190,000 for every person in the country. Germany and France each clock in at less than $4.5 trillion, representing 1.6 and 2.1 times GDP respectively. The IMF guide suggests this figure should not be over 2.5 times GDP.

There is no doubt that the UK economy is seriously over borrowed and weaker than comparable western economies with whom we trade. China and India have external debt amounting to just over 5% of GDP. The figures tell us that the UK is even less well placed than similar sized economies in Europe and our special partner, the US, none of which are problem free. Indeed the UK position could become precarious, as these are statistics at the start of the coming recession, not at its end.

3

A feature of this global crisis has been the vulnerability of financial institutions. In the UK our financial companies, namely banks, building societies, life assurance and pensions companies had been very strong in the past, weathering the great depression and two world wars as well as the various post war economic troughs. Even in the 1970's it was only the fringe banks and maverick insurance companies that went down. The main pillars of the financial system remained firm. Not this time. Why?

We need now to consider four elements. These are the nature of assets, the nature of debt, the purpose of income, the value of capital and their relationship with each other in a financially sound structure. We need also to define the difference between investing and speculating. We need to do this, because it is the distortion of these elements and their relationship with us that is at the root of much that has gone wrong. Moreover failure to grasp the reality of these issues will set us on a path to recovery that will take us over a cliff. Quite simply the country will risk going bust.

Let us begin with debt. Money owed remains constant until paid. Its value does not fluctuate and if secured against an asset, movements in the valuation of the asset have no effect on the debt. On the other hand, the value of an asset is to an extent illusory, because if many similar assets come on the market together, or if there are few or no buyers, the value falls.

Asset valuation is by nature historic and should serve as a guide of potential liquidity but not as a basis of the determination of an absolute financial position. Loans secured against assets will remain an outstanding liability to the borrower at the full face value whatever happens to the value of the asset. Equally, asset based matching of future liabilities such as pension payments, will offer no guarantee that funds will be in readiness to meet them. The way to avoid problems is to match liabilities to assets with a guaranteed maturity at the point at which the cash will me needed, of which government gilt edged stock is considered the safest choice.

The income which assets provide, which may affect asset value because of its growth or shrinkage, is nevertheless of a different character. Whether in the form of dividend, rent or interest it is paid independently and does not require the sale of part of the asset to pay it. Income or yield was once the governing factor in determining the worth of an asset to the investor. Now growth potential is too often the measure.

Income traditionally formed the basis of premium calculation for pensions and life assurance. Cautious actuaries used an interest assumption of 2.5% pa in setting premium rates and pension fund managers used a high proportion of gilts in their portfolios to guarantee the security of their funds. This insulated pensioners and savers from the economic cycle and made the financial institutions secure from the effects of what we now call market turmoil.

Unfortunately this cautious approach is more costly as it requires much larger funds to deliver, with certainty, the projected outcome, but the saver enjoys rock solid guarantees that his savings are safe. New concepts began to appear in the sixties and seventies that relied on growth in asset value rather than income and did away with the expensive guarantees. The result is the transfer of the risk from the institution to the saver, so that if asset values fall, the saver will have less. Such an approach accords well with the free market philosophy and works if asset values keep rising. In the event of a crash it is the saver who suffers. Suddenly we hear about pension black holes.

For the saver this is very unsatisfactory. The institution with its investment skill is within its legal duty if it declares to the pensioner that his fund is worth a fraction of what was projected and has no obligation to meet the expectations offered at the time the plan was begun. It is however why constant reference is nowadays made to pension fund deficits and pensioners suffering in adverse markets. Under the old system both the institution and the saver are safe in financial turmoil short of national bankruptcy.

The ever more demanding quest for growth in asset values has led to a tendency for assets to grow without reference to any corresponding improvement in their yield in far too many cases. I was taught that the starting yield of a newly purchased share should be not less than 3.5% and yield on property 6%. Any acceleration of value reducing the opening yield would indicate an over valued asset which would eventually have to be corrected by a price fall. The riskier nature of the investment, the higher the yield must be.

Unfortunately in the drift towards chasing accelerating asset values, three things happened. First a new generation of investment analysts and managers began to ignore income and concentrate on growth in share or property (or commodity) values, pushing their values up, leaving balance sheets, pension and savings funds and even banks vulnerable to a serious market reverse.

Second, asset inflation especially in residential property, created a sense of wealth which could only be realised by borrowing against the equity in the property. Soon the price of property inflated well beyond its realistic value and purchasing a home involved an excessive proportion of annual income. This left nothing over, leading to more borrowing.

Third, banks fuelled the borrowing binge by lending much more than they had attracted from savers. In the past the two elements, money lent and deposits received, had to more or less balance and be supported by strong capital reserves in the banks. After 2000 banks became less and less attentive to the old rules and began to borrow extensively from international markets, so as to lend more and more. In the end some £700 billion has been borrowed by banks over and above their deposits. This is why two went bust and had to be nationalised, three others needed major recapitalisation with taxpayers' money and one has had to become part owned by oil producers in the Middle East.

Therefore, of the three pillars of our financial structure, on which in past crises we had been able to rely as the bedrock of stability, two, the banks and building societies became vulnerable and in some cases unstable. The third, the life assurance and pensions companies, have remained largely unscathed because by changes in product design over the last twenty years, most of them transferred the risk to their policyholders, who have seen their savings shrink and who have no guarantees to fall back on. Those companies still offering the guarantees appear to have stuck to the old rules.

Most critical of all is the whereabouts of the pebbles, in grown up terms, the currency reserves. Starting with where they are not, if we take the US, the UK and the Eurozone together we find only an astonishing 8% of the total. If we take China and Russia together we find over 30%. If we add Hong Kong and Taiwan and India to that total we reach nearly 42%. Japan, Korea, Singapore, Malaysia and the Philippines together, we find another 20%.

The political effect long term of this shift of financial power will be seen by history as comparable, indeed greater, than the power shifts which occurred as a consequence of the world wars of the twentieth century. It represents a strategic defeat for the West which is both functional as well as ideological. The Western economic model lies in ruins as powerful symbolically as the rubble of Berlin in 1945. Essentially the West has run out of money. The statement that the banking system has 'seized up' is a euphemism for the stark fact that the countries who now hold the cash are no longer willing to lend it as they think they might lose it. They think we might go bust. They may be right.

Whether we are able to dig ourselves out of our financial rubble will depend on whether those responsible for leading their people to this disaster, have the wit and humility to see the error of their ways and a plan of how the economic structure should be more securely rebuilt. To stimulate the economy of the UK by a revival of consumer borrowing and a new surge in the residential property market will lead quite simply to national bankruptcy. If repeated in the US this will lead to a complete systemic collapse of the western financial structure.

4

To avert complete disaster in the greatest financial crisis in modern history, will require courage and skill of the kind needed to traverse a tricky ridge on the side of a mountain. One slip and you are gone. The worrying aspect of the whole situation is that none in authority seemed to realise where we were headed before the start of the crunch. Worse, when we got there nobody seemed sure where we were. People learn fast and we must hope they get it right. In order to judge the likely success of whatever actions unfold and, more important, whether they could lead to even more trouble, it is useful to set some fundamentals down now. The UK economy, which is the most vulnerable in the West, must be completely rebalanced.

This will be a major undertaking that could take up to a generation to complete. There will be no quick fix. At the base of our national economy we must have absolutely sound financial institutions. There must be free markets also and within those there will always be speculators and bubbles that burst. This is a major part of the UK's economic activity and it is a world class player. These markets must be free to innovate and function without crippling regulation, but they must be underpinned by a rock solid financial core. There will always be an economic cycle and market dives, but these troughs should be capable of being absorbed as part of the economic progress.

Banks must urgently rebuild sound balance sheets that can weather economic storms and this will be more likely if banks go back to being banks, which are supposed to borrow short from their depositors and lend short to business and industry to keep the wheels of commerce turning. This is vital if people are to have well paid jobs and spare income to spend in the High Street. Banks should not major on house purchase finance or consumer lending.

Building Societies must enjoy a revival and take up the job of providing long term finance for people who wish to buy their homes. We must revive the system where the interest rate was set at the outset for the life of the mortgage, so that borrowers know where they stand and can plan their finances in a stable environment. Above all we must bring house prices under control so that the value of the average house is no greater than three and a half times the average wage. This adjustment will take time but we must reach the point where ever increasing proportions of consumer spending is with ready, not borrowed, money.

Life assurance and Pensions companies need to be revived to provide secure forms of regular saving for the long term, with a substantial part of the outcome guaranteed. The practice of regular saving for retirement and a rainy day, lost in the glitter of gold plastic as a key to need, has resulted in a nation of net savers becoming a nation of net spenders. Go into the forest and talk to a squirrel if you do not understand that this is a bad idea.

We must overcome the convention that everyone must own their home. Of course it is a good idea for many, the majority even, but there is a major place for a ready supply of rented property. This provides better mobility of labour and prevents wild surges in residential property prices undermining the whole economy. Private landlords, struggling with mortgages, though a useful element perhaps, are vulnerable and not ideal. Pension funds and insurance companies should be encouraged to create good quality portfolios of rented property and a proper maintenance service to tenants to ensure that a substantial proportion of residential property, especially in cities and large towns can be rented without fear of exploitation by unscrupulous or incompetent landlords.

Local authorities must be allowed to start rebuilding their housing stock. Most important, they must be allowed to keep the proceeds of sales to reinvest in more housing. There is no reason why private landlords should not sell to tenants or offer shared equity schemes.

They keep the proceeds of such sales for further investment and to refuse this benefit to local authorities in present circumstances is socially unhelpful, and financially unsound.

Sound financial institutions, a more rational approach to housing, a more reliable yardstick by which to judge asset value, less consumer borrowing, more long term saving with a greater certainty of outcome and recognition that there is more to an economy than an overheated housing market, all provide firm principles by which to rebuild the finances of our nation.

Immediately ahead, there are grim events to unfold. Insolvencies, bankruptcies, unemployment, repossessions are all predicted to rise. In human terms this means shattered lives, broken dreams, fear and despair. How to ease the path of the people through this coming dark time will be at the front of every politician's mind. It is the duty of the government to play its part. What should that part be?

5

This is when the going becomes muddied by political ideology, more government or less, free markets or economic plans and so on. Let us try to avoid the trap of supposing that one of the old isms has the answer. All have been tried and none lived up to expectations, though maybe all achieved something. What we now need is a practical approach.

Such is the level of personal debt in the UK that any quick fix by encouraging it to rise further, is absolutely out of the question. A reduction in interest rates is a good thing if it helps business and helps consumers to reduce their level of debt, the latter being an absolute priority. It is a bad thing for encouraging savings, another priority, and a total disaster if it starts another credit surge. There is also a risk of too greater fall in the value of sterling. Although a cheaper pound helps exporters, it also increases the cost of foreign debt. With 3.5 times our GDP owed overseas, this is an important factor.

The plain fact, unpleasant though facing it will be, is that any recovery must be based on consumers spending a far higher proportion of their own money, whilst setting enough aside for future security. There is a powerful case for the inflation target of the Bank of England to include housing and for the mortgage rate to be officially decoupled from bank rate. To a large extend this has happened in practice but the task ought should be given to the Bank of setting an official mortgage rate quite separately to bank rate, to enable it to control house price inflation. Had this single power been given at the time it was given the responsibility to manage inflation by controlling interest rates, we would not be in the current crisis.

In the old days of fiscal control it was quite normal for varying credit conditions to apply to different parts of the market and the supposition that one interest rate set is all you need for so diverse a spread of circumstances is be too simplistic. To suppose that you can have rampant inflation in housing while there is negligible inflation in the rest of the economy without the bubble bursting, is as irrational as to suppose you can sunbathe in a thunderstorm. The idea that it creates wealth is illusory. The actual long term result, as we now see, is a vast increase in personal debt.

The Bank of England needs to have its remit extended to monitor the expansion of consumer credit and should call in special deposits from banks if interest rates alone are not providing sufficient weight. External debt must be brought down to 2.5% of GDP then reduced to 2%. This will take time but, make no mistake; it has to happen if any recovery is to be more than a flash in the pan.

The government will have to be proactive in cutting a path through the mess. There are those who believe that all that is necessary is to reduce interest rates and give tax cuts and everything will work out. All that will happen is that there will be an illusion of recovery, rather like after a hefty dose of analgesic in the midst of a bout of 'flu makes you feel better so you go back to work, but the day of reckoning comes, only worse. You could get pneumonia and die, especially if you were a bit frail to start with. We have to face the hard fact that our financial structure in these islands is now frail.

A good figure for the UK is inward investment, known as FDI (foreign direct investment) and is the measure of how much each country has accumulated in terms of foreign firms putting money into business and industry within the receiving country. At the top of the list is the USA with just over $ 2 trillion. Next comes the UK with $ 1.35 trillion and although dwarfed by the $ 10 trillion we owe overseas, it is a positive measure of how favourably foreign investors judge the UK business environment, which is good for our economy and provides employment. To put the figure into context China with its massive growth enjoys about a quarter of the UK level at just over $300 billion.

This is a strength we need to preserve and develop. The countries of the East with the money, now so cautious about lending it, may still be encouraged to invest. It will not be as before. Those cash rich countries have, in most cases, huge opportunities for developing their own internal infrastructure and social amenities and will judge now a good time to concentrate on raising the standards of life for their own people. If we ensure that we continue to offer mobility and flexibility of labour, a good taxation regime and improvements to our own infrastructure, there will still be opportunities to attract investment, even if there is less of it around.

It may not be right to make an inflexible case against limited government borrowing as a means of helping the economy out of recession, but how much and what for are absolutely critical questions. The issue of debt size, as every household knows, is very much related to income, because it is the income which services the debt and pays it off. If you run up debts with a static income or one which is falling you may find yourself looking bailiffs in the eye when things get out of hand. If your income rises, as long as you are sensible all will be well. Any government borrowing must have a positive effect on its own income from tax revenues increasing and must add value to the economy.

If the government now borrows and the result is another credit binge, international bailiffs in the form of the IMF will surely arrive. We suffered that humiliation and all the pain in the 1970's with consequences that went on into the 1980's. It is therefore extremely important that Government uses borrowing wisely. The problem with focussing almost exclusively on the retail economy, which is the current practice, is that it puts the emphasis too far forward in the chain of events that lead to spending. There then remains the risk that in kick starting the economy, as the saying goes, there is a trip into a credit surge.

Any stimulus should therefore concentrate on the root and not be wasted on quick fixes. If we are to remain a competitive trading and manufacturing nation, which is what we are, we need to have the infrastructure and communications to match, which rival the best in the world. We also need the best schools and hospitals. We need mobility and flexibility of labour and a fiscal structure that encourages enterprise but rewards thrift. Above all we must have a sound financial base and a strong exporting industrial and technological sector.

If the government now gives priority to the rebuilding of schools and hospitals, new rail projects linking regions and cities with high speed lines, as well as environmental projects such as flood defences, with a general object of renewing what is, in parts of the country especially the South, a creaking infrastructure, it will be laying the foundation for a great renewal of economic strength. It cannot do this on its own and the private sector will have great opportunities.

It will also create jobs paying people real money for doing real work which will have a positive impact on the future prospects of our country for generations to come. There must be a shakeout of coordinators, facilitators and snoopers. There must be fewer meetings with fewer people at them. Individual responsibility must be revived and a reliance on practice and procedure reduced. People must be trained to do a real job, not taught to follow the letter of a manual.

The opportunities are enormous for the private sector, and for government, are almost endless. Climate change gives a new urgency to modernization of motor vehicles so that most become environmentally neutral through hybrid technology. Old branch lines can be opened and refurbished for rail busses to provide fast and environmentally efficient links to country areas reducing the reliance on motor transport. Better handling facilities at more ports with enhanced rail connections will enable goods to be exported or landed nearer to the point of manufacture or destination.

We need to remind ourselves that our industrial revolution came about because of our ability to transport goods first by canal and then by rail from anywhere to anywhere in our country. Our empire, which was of trade rather than conquest, was founded on our vast shipping fleet and the railways we built overseas. The laxity with which we have overlooked these lessons of history exacts the telling price of our current predicament and accounts for the fact that short of flying it now mostly takes longer to get from A to B in our country than it did in the 1930's.

Another aim must be to repatriate both currency and jobs from overseas. We have a substantial industrial base in all the key industries and technologies. It is to the regeneration of this economic core that we must now direct more effort. The government can provide the framework and the stimulus organising infrastructure renewal and enterprise initiatives. The goal must be to reduce debt and in future earn a much higher proportion of what we spend and to save more of what we earn. There is no secure future in new kitchens and funky clothes bought with plastic money. They are the topping at the end. They do not make a meal.

6

Last in this chapter I come to taxation, in particular income tax. I have left it till last because it is a key to future success. The whole system is over complicated and unfair. The time has come for major reform. Not tinkering reform that politicians talk about but nobody else can see or understand. Root and branch stuff.

The last major reform took place in the early days of the first Thatcher government when there was a giant shift from tax on incomes to tax on spending. At that point income tax had reached exotic levels of up to 95% at the top end and in the mid 30's at the bottom. Clearly this was unsatisfactory and the new government introduced major cuts in income tax, but at the same time doubled vat on spending. The consensus then and since is that this was fairer and encouraged enterprise.

The problem is that the impact of income tax is much higher for the low paid than for the higher earners, because they are also paying tax on all the essentials of life except food from their small income. You cannot have it both ways. You cannot tax your lowest earners on their incomes and their spending. All you do is reduce their spending and

43

make their lives harder. Worse you drive them into borrowing.

Well, they should earn more, you say. But that is not productive, as you will have to pay dinner ladies £30,000 a year and hospital cleaners £40,000. I exaggerate to make the point but a vibrant, cohesive economy needs to treat its low earners fairly. Moreover these jobs are critical to the functioning of society and are vital for the economy. We cannot function as a nation of bankers, lawyers and celebrities.

Sensing this, governments have introduced one relief after another trying to target this group and that, often causing confusion and hampered by dysfunctional computer programmes costing taxpayers hundreds of millions. In the end there is a sullen resignation, a switching off, a live for today approach, a distrust of politicians.

We know from experience in the years of very high taxation on the top earners that it is more of a political gesture than a working economic model, as the revenue actually collected is less. A tax avoidance industry is set up with all kinds of devices to reduce the amount of tax paid. Making the better off pay more through higher rates above certain levels does not really work. It seems unfair to respond by overtaxing the low paid. This is because low paid earners have to pay tax which comes out of their income for essentials, whereas higher paid earners have tax eat into their luxury potential. The incentive to do better is useful, but the penalty must not begin too early. The figures make the point.

Using round figures and ignoring the latest adjustments to stimulate the economy, the single person's allowance is £6030. Such a person on £15000 pays tax at 20% on £8970. This amounts to £1794 or £149.50 per month. If we make a general assumption that this person has basic living costs to include, rent, fuel travel to work etc of £900 per month, this leaves on the gross income of £1250 per month a sum of £ 350 for everything else including quite possibly food and clothes. If we now deduct the tax of £133 per month from the surplus over the fixed living costs it comes out at a rate of 38%. If we do the same sums on a £40000 per year earner, with the same basic living costs the rate works out at 23%.

If we use the same figures after basic living costs, the recent emergency reduction in vat puts and extra £5.42 per month into the pocket of the lower earner and £50.42 per month for the higher earner in the two examples above. This gives us a clue of what is wrong. It is the case that indirect tax can be fairer for all only if low earners do not have to bear the burden of income tax as well. A reduction disproportionately helps the higher earner and spender. The converse is true. Raising vat from 17.5% to 20% would cost the low earner an extra £5.42 and the higher earner £50.42. Neither of these figures is likely to kick start the economy or drive it deeper into recession.

The answer is bold and dramatic. A high personal allowance that takes the low paid out of tax altogether, a single rate of tax and an increase in vat.

There are only four components to such a system.

1 A personal allowance that takes all low paid workers out of income tax altogether.

2 A single tax rate on income, paid by everyone on all income over the personal allowance.

3 VAT as we know it today.

4 The fading of the personal allowance for higher earners.

The combination works together as a package, but is almost infinitely flexible, as the rate for each component can be varied. I am not going to attempt to recommend rates appropriate to current or future conditions as I am only concerned with the principle in this book, but I will give an illustration to explain the idea.

Set the personal allowance to £15000, taking all lower paid workers out of income altogether. This puts an extra £1794 into the pockets of this deserving group, or £149.50 per month.

Increase vat to 20%. This would cost, over the normal rate of 17.5%, an extra £8.75 per month if applied to the surplus over the basic living cost of a £15000 per year earner. This shows the taxpayer to be very much better off.

Set the single tax rate at 24% on all taxable income over the personal allowance of £15000. The lowest paid pay nothing and all other taxpayers are a little better off. Those on £30000 gain £63 per month and those on £40,000 gain £14 per month. If we fade the personal allowance pound for pound from £85000, those on £100000 are £426 per month in pocket. This assumes everyone has the same basic living cost of £9000 which is either vat free or on special rates and takes account of the fact that no vat is paid on income tax.

Depending on the willingness of the government to borrow to fund the reform, the outcome can be changed by altering one or more of any of the four components. To see what happens with an increase in the income tax rate I tried 30%. The low paid are unaffected, the £30000 earner loses£10.75 per month, the £40000 £107 and the £100000 £46. Each comparison is with the recently current two rate system, personal allowance and vat at 17.5% and relates to all income after the basic living cost. Neither of the new proposals is compared to the other but the sum is easy to do.

A point worth making is that the system has its equilibrium in the middle, with middle earners. By easing the burden on the lowest paid very significantly we have left the middle earners in much the same position and we have increased the spending power of the highest earners. This increased spending power at the top end directly assists the low end helping to offset the cost of raising the personal allowance, but the middle earners suffer no adverse effects.

This is the direct opposite of the approach currently used. The removal of an extra (or now two extra) tax bands will avoid schemes to wriggle out of tax liabilities. The lack of tax liability of low paid workers will reduce the administrative burden for small businesses employing part time staff. The ending of all the peculiar credits and other devices to mask the inequity of the present system will save millions in costs.

A final caution about where the money comes from. There are doubtless many economies which can be made, but politicians tend to exaggerate potential savings at the margin and then prove reluctant to axe expensive programmes which would make real savings, because of the effect on jobs in the wider economy. Wars on waste, like wars on terror, are hard to define, difficult to prosecute and end in an outcome which is either a stalemate or a compromise. Our tax system has to deliver the revenue the country requires to run the society we want and we must face up to what that really costs and pay up.

Dancing through a thicket of stealth taxes, credits, benefits and incentives may conceal from us what is going on, but in the end we pay. Better to walk steadily down a straight path and know where we are. What is needed is to be fair when collecting and to have a keen eye on the impact of taxation and what it achieves rather than looking at headline figures, which turn out to be so misleading. If economic circumstances force the country to have higher taxes than it would like, the burden must not fall on those least well off. Lower paid workers should not have to apply for complex credits and benefits to beg relief. It is inequitable, hugely costly to administer and bad for the economy as a whole.

7

Most of this chapter was written before the full impact of the financial crisis developed. I have avoided revision as much as possible as to alter the analysis with hindsight is to devalue it; instead of being an independent assessment it would become another report. There are now emerging three critical issues which must be resolved if any recovery is to be lasting and not the briefest of booms between one crisis and the next.

The first is the level of government debt. This is now widely recognised by those who stop to think, as beyond anything previously imagined and utterly unsustainable. If a Zimbabwe type ending to this calamitous financial experience is to be avoided two things will be needed; a massive cut in public spending and a significant increase in overall taxation. Unfortunately those charged with the task of dealing with this, politicians, believe that either element on its own can lead to electoral disaster and together they form a dual carriageway to electoral oblivion. The government asserts that spending will continue to rise. If true, which is unlikely, this would amount to lunacy.

The opposition parties proclaim spending to be out of control, but have not yet come forward with other than nuggets of improved housekeeping to explain how they will, if elected, resolve the matter. The public may not be as faint hearted as their leaders, for whom they now have little respect. It may very well be that they would prefer a period of dramatic austerity as a means to national solvency, rather than tottering debt ridden from one national financial emergency to another.

The next, in some ways even more alarming, is the mounting problem of public service pensions. The U.S has a big problem here as its public service pensions are projected to reach twenty five per cent of GDP. In the U.K ours will reach eighty five per cent of GDP. This is completely off the page, cannot happen, will not be paid and someone has to bite the bullet and own up to the impossibility of this commitment. To continue to make contractual promises to public servants, which have no realistic prospects of fulfilment, amounts to little better than fraud.

We indeed have a double pension crisis, because even those in the private sector find their final salary schemes are being frozen and withdrawn. This is largely because of the failure to use a proper basis of valuing funds. Switching from a yield based valuation to one based on current market asset values has effectively destroyed the private pension structure in the U.K, previously a main pillar of the economy. From now on consumers will have to spend a great deal less and save a good deal more. The implications of this need to be properly thought through, as an economic model that expects the working population to spend its spare time shopping may not fit future circumstances at all.

There is no word that hereafter will conjure so much agitation and dismay as *bonus,* especially if relating to those working in banks or financial services. Many of these bonuses relate to profits expressed in the share price of the company. This is a repeat of the problem which destroyed the viability of the pension funds. Bonuses calculated this way will go to the wrong people for the wrong reasons, as we have seen in largest measure to those who actually bust their banks. Changing the calculation to a sustainable yield formula would help. Valuing a share not at the current market figure but a three and a half per cent yield on the actual dividend averaged over three or five years would drive the reward to those earning real sustainable money for their company.

There is a final statistic which is worrying if correct. I heard it said recently that twenty years ago the average Chief executive's pay was fifteen times the average of the workforce of that business. It is now apparently of seventy times. This is, if true, very unsatisfactory. Of course there should be reward for effort and risk. There must nevertheless be a clear line between reward and greed.

8

Blueprint

1 **We must rebalance the economy to put it on a firmer footing.** Trying to get out of the recession with Government borrowing to boost retail spending in the short term is very dangerous. There is no guarantee that it will work and much High Street spending is on imported goods. We must accept that we cannot have an economy sustained by house price inflation and ever expanding credit.

2 **There must be more saving and less borrowing.** Saving must offer security to savers and a fair return. This is the contrary to the need for low interest rates and requires a decoupling of saver rates from bank rate. This would be possible if banks concentrated on shot term lending for business and building societies reclaimed the mortgage market and deposit savings.

3 **The underlying strength of all our financial institutions needs to be more secure.**
Asset valuations for long term investment must return to a yield rather than a growth or market basis. Balance sheets of

institutions which declare asset values at current market price are utterly unrealistic. Capital ratios need to improve. There is scope for re-mutualising some building societies which became banks. This could be extended to some insurance companies, especially life assurance and pensions.

4 **Long term savings products such as pensions must be secured with guarantees** and supported by matched investment mainly of gilts. This will create a useful demand for Government stock from within the UK and encourage saving for the longer term financial security.

5 **Income tax must be reformed** to make it an effective instrument of fiscal management not a tool of social engineering. Low earners must come out of income tax altogether.

6 **Over time house prices must adjust to become affordable** without excessive mortgages. House price rises must be included in the Bank of England's remit to control inflation. Consideration should be given to having an official Mortgage Rate as well as Bank Rate to allow targeted monetary control.

7 **The Bank of England should have its remit widened to include maintaining sustainable debt levels**, not just through interest rates but through special deposits from retail banks.

8 **Pension funds, insurance companies and large property companies should be encouraged to invest in good quality residential property to rent**, especially in urban areas to increase the flexibility of labour and to provide effective competition to home ownership. This will have a stabilising effect on the housing market and take up unsold developments and developments in progress as well as boosting the construction industry.

9 **Government borrowing must be targeted at facilitating long term renewal** not short term stimulus and be kept within manageable limits. The aim must be to return to budget surpluses as the country and world emerge from the recession. Resources must accumulate for support in the next downturn. Public funds should rarely be used to bail out debt.

10 **We must redevelop our industrial base to make more of what we buy** so as to reduce foreign debt and increase our currency reserves. This will mean encouraging inward

investment and may require initial government funding. If this is done with preference shares rather than loans, the taxpayer will be repaid out of the sale of the shares when the business is developed, rather on the lines of the privatisations of the eighties. We need to make more of the small ticket consumer items for everyday use.

11 It may be necessary to introduce a transferable loan to cover negative equity. House prices need to fall by about 50% from the peak to rebalance the economy on a sounder footing. This will leave very large numbers of households in negative equity, unable to move home. An endowment based guarantee scheme could easily be devised to enable the negative element to be transferred from house to house as a second charge, to be paid off by the end of the term of the original mortgage. This would be to some extent offset for the home owner by the significantly lower cost of the new home.

12 Nationalising the basic banking system may be a necessity, including the retail infrastructure and the traditional banking service to business and consumers. The bailout of the so called investment banking arms and their toxic debts is wrong. These assets are valueless and the instruments without reality outside markets dealing in what became fantasy. There is no way that the taxpayer should be saddled with this shambles and those responsible must learn that the price for alchemy is ruin. If we saddle the taxpayer with this burden the poor will be funding the recovery of the rich.

2010
A Blueprint for Change
Part 2
Chapters 9-15

Foreign Policy

In this chapter our relationship with the United States is a central theme. For far too long our foreign policy has been crafted to maintain the so called Special Relationship, without properly defining what this is supposed to be. Certainly we have a relationship with the country which was once a collection of our Colonies and whose founders all had roots in these islands. But is the U.S what it would have us believe? What faults lie forgotten in the tectonic plates of its origins? Whilst assessing the future of our foreign policy we need to revisit some unhappy issues of the past.

9

Traditionally British Foreign policy was crafted to support the weakest coalition of powers against the strongest in Europe and, once a start had been made on building the empire, to expand our power everywhere else. This worked against Napoleon in the end, though it was a lengthy business. The empire was built with surprising little conflict. Sea power, rather than a large land army, appropriate for an island nation, was both the means of protection and projection.

The most successful period of this model of diplomacy was in the century following the defeat of Napoleon at Waterloo. There Wellington lead an army of many nations, but his principal ally was Prussia, whose forces made a comeback after being defeated earlier and arrived to support Wellington in the nick of time. For ninety-nine years thereafter we were engaged in relatively minor conflicts, mainly the Crimea and the Boer War. Europe was largely at peace. Then in 1914 we were at war again, but this time our protestant ally Prussia, now the leader of the German Empire, was our enemy, and our traditional enemy, France, was our ally. The scale of the carnage which followed was up till then beyond all imagination.

The drift away from our natural ally in Europe, Germany, towards our traditional enemy, France, was a response to the former's increasing military and industrial power, in particular the development of a modern navy. By siding with France through the entente cordiale the balance on continental Europe was restored. At least that was the rationale at the time. It was also the case that Germany was ruled by an autocratic monarchy and was not, unlike France and Great Britain, a democracy. Moreover there was a good deal of evidence that the Kaiser was not altogether sane.

Balances of power work only if war is avoided. History's most successful example is the Cold War. Had that become a hot war, none of you would have been here to read these words, nor I to write them. The Cold War taught us that the essence of balance is deterrence. No country can win. All will be destroyed.

Unfortunately this was not quite so clear cut before the invention of nuclear weapons, which are at the same time both a great blessing if their very existence keeps the peace, but the most terrible nightmare if they are used. Sadly for the millions slaughtered, the issues in 1914 were not so stark, because the effect of the weapons technology of the time was not understood. Essentially this gave the balance of advantage to defence over attack.

Had the generals of the day studied the American Civil War in depth they would have seen the portents, but these seem to have been overlooked on all sides. While Germany, with superior forces, managed a convincing victory on its eastern front, in the west things were different. Until the treaty of Brest Litovsk the German imperative was to hold its ground in France and Belgium in the west. The allied imperative was to break through and throw the Germans back. This they failed to do. The casualties were on a scale that turned war into slaughter. Finally Germany launched its great offensive in 1918 which failed, thus creating the opportunity for a successful allied counter offensive which ended the war.

The challenging thought is that had Britain been allied with Germany, the war in the west would have been over before the end of 1914. There would have been no military balance. France would have been unable to withstand the German advance on its own in 1914 any more than it did in 1876. It is likely that there would not have been the Nazis, the Holocaust, or the Second World War. Millions would have been left alive. We need to remember that the

Germany of 1914 was not the tyrannical juggernaut of 1939. Certainly it was not a democracy yet, but to get there was surely not worth the carnage.

Thus it is possible to argue that by changing alliances for reasons which may have misjudged the potential military consequences, we in these islands unwittingly contributed to the disasters of the twentieth century. The Entente Cordiale was signed in 1904. It was followed by two world wars and a military/ ideological stand off, which between them occupied almost the whole of the twentieth century. That is not to say the move was definitely wrong. Neither does it tell us that it was definitely right. What it does tell us is that war is no longer a feasible means of resolving issues between states, except perhaps on a localised scale. It also tells us that one war, instead of ending wars, can create the very conditions which lead to another.

Here at the start of the twenty first century we need to look at our foreign policy in the light of a changing world. Mostly since the end of the Second World War and certainly since Suez, British foreign policy has been largely that of the United States with which we enjoy, as we are told, a Special Relationship. This is an odd term which though understood, is hard to explain. It stems in no small measure, I suspect, from our loss of influence and empire after 1945 and a desire to remain at the topmost table of world affairs.

It may be that a subconscious understanding of the ultimate outcome of joining the weaker coalition pre 1914, led to a later motivation to join the strongest, to make the combination invincible. Although the US is a superpower, if you add our economy to it and all our armed forces including our nuclear deterrent, the result is a military and economic mega power, which has had its own way (the only major fissure is over climate change) since the end of the cold war. It was trouble in our two economies that brought on the global financial crisis. Without the consumer borrowing binge in the US and UK and the reckless conduct of their joint financial institutions, there would be no world crisis.

The special relationship means to the rest of the world that our two nations, sharing language, culture and heritage, though separate, are more together than any other major countries on earth. It is a combination which the U.S sees as for the universal good, we never much think about, whilst others are not so sure. Before we explore whether we should once again have a foreign policy which is tailored to the needs and interests of these islands, which may be different in emphasis as well as substance from that of the U.S, we need to take a closer look at the country which is America. Individual Americans are at once the most generous, most welcoming, most ready to listen, most open, most innovative people on earth. Unhappily their country collectively does not always live up their example when conducting itself overseas.

10

America began hesitantly with settlers both French and British but the British became dominant. Eventually the British colonists quarrelled with the home Government, declared independence and after winning a war which the British bungled, became fully independent in 1776. The founding fathers, as these victorious colonists came to be known, set about turning their colonies into countries, calling them States.

At this point we need to pause for a moment and consider the nature of what had happened. This was not a rebellion by an indigenous people against a conquering power. This was a rebellion by conquerors against their home government. The indigenous people of the country they were colonising, the Native Americans, then known as Red Indians, were not party to these events at all. Indeed their ultimate fate is a stain on the American claim to champion the rights of the free.

The colonists gained independence to proceed with their ambitions for a new country unfettered by control from a central government thousands of miles to the east. They set to work founding an advanced republican democracy in which the separate States were autonomous but joined together in a continental union collectively called the United States of America.

There were some issues. The two most divisive were that, first, though the constitution was founded on the premise that all men (people) were equal, this excluded the large population of black slaves. The second problem was that there was disagreement as to whether the union of the states was voluntary with final sovereignty remaining with the individual State, or whether the union once made was indivisible and final sovereignty rested with the Union. These two issues combined to form a fatal combustion when seventy two years after the election of George Washington to be the first President, the election of Abraham Lincoln to be the sixteenth, caused the Union to fracture and led to a terrible civil war.

More books have been published about the American Civil War than any other event in history I am told, so I shall not dwell upon it here in any length. There are nevertheless some key points worth exploring. The first and the worst is the death toll. Six hundred thousand lives were lost in this terrible conflict, a telling rebuke to the efficacy of the durability of this new republic. Yet in paradox it survived and renewed itself, its institutions intact or shortly restored and went on to become the richest and most powerful nation on earth.

One institution did not survive. Slavery was finally abolished. Freeing the slaves became the reason for the war. It made the horrific death toll somehow more acceptable. It gave the sacrifice a noble cause. Many people still believe the war was about slavery but that is no truer than saying the European Union is about the Euro.

Abraham Lincoln said in August 1862, sixteen months into the war

'My paramount objective in this struggle is to save the Union, and is not either to save or destroy slavery. If I could save the Union without freeing any slave I would do it. If I could save it by freeing all the slaves I would do it; and if I could save it by freeing some and leaving others alone I would do that'.

That leaves no doubt or ambiguity. The terrible struggle was over the issue of whether individual states had the right to leave the Union and organise themselves in a different grouping or not. This would naturally include their right to continue to hold black people in bondage. The eleven

Southern states which seceded believed they had the right to leave a voluntary union to which they no longer wished to belong.

Lincoln and the Republican Party, which had carried all the Northern states in the election, believed they had not. The war was about the right of people to determine the nature of their government and their institutions, or better perhaps, having chosen previously, to change their minds. The position of the United States at that time, has made its later declarations on matters connected with the right of free peoples to determine their future, appear to its friends rather cynical and to its enemies quite dishonest.

Seen in those terms, the war loses a good deal of its nobility. The aspirations of the South were crushed by brute force in an unequal match, leaving a century of inequality for African Americans. We can be sure that had the Confederacy been allowed its independence, slavery would have ended sooner or later by the sheer force of world opinion. Had it ended without such terrible bloodshed with its legacy of bitterness in the South, maybe black people would have been given better prospects with their freedom.

What we cannot know is whether two republics could have co-habited the American continent without conflict erupting at some point. We may need therefore to accept Lincoln's proposition that the Union was critical to the cohesive survival of the American vision and acknowledge that the civil war welded the Union so that the dream of the founding fathers ultimately could be fulfilled. Whether that justified six hundred thousand Americans killing each other is open to question and if it did, shows a terrible failure in the workings of democracy.

This is the key. It is the fault in the tectonic plates of America's foundations, for the Unites States was not framed as a united kingdom, but as a democratic union of free colonies, now called states. It was to be the world's most advanced and by definition, most perfect, democracy. However, it is the essence of democracy that a people has the right to decide not only the complexion of its government, but its nature. The people also have the power, through the exercise of their democratic rights, to choose with whom they conjoin or unite. Democracy is not just about the who in government, it is about the how and with whom as well.

It is also a fact of democracy that one generation cannot bind the next. It can only bequeath. The new generation has the right to change not only anything but everything. If the United States was a true democracy, the decision of the people of one or several states to decide to leave that Union and form a separate grouping, cannot be stopped. It cannot be said to be rebellion. It cannot be said to be treason. It is the exercise of the fundamental human right of self determination.

Lincoln's policy to subjugate the Confederacy by force was without democratic legitimacy and by the very act declared that America was not in the true sense a democracy. The South was fighting for its independence. Lincoln's interpretation was that once made, the Union was unbreakable, to challenge it was rebellion. The moral and ethical deficiency of this position was politically repaired by the adherence of the South to slavery. Having not had the abolition of slavery as an initial war aim, Lincoln shrewdly introduced it when it was likely that without it he would lose. Had there been no such thing as slavery in America, it is unlikely that Lincoln would be revered by history, or even Americans, as he is today. Some may say there would have been no war, but that is by no means certain. The rift of which had the final power, State or Union ran very deep.

A strange irony is that had the American colonies not rebelled against Great Britain and won their independence, slavery would have ended in 1834 with the coming into force of the Abolition of Slavery Act, freeing all slaves throughout the British Empire, some thirty years earlier and without recourse to war. Indeed slaves were freed all over the civilised world without provoking war.

What is so disturbing about this convulsion in the birth of the United States is the savagery of the conquest of the South. Grant and Sherman, who between them won the war for the Union (and without whom the Union might not have prevailed), asserted that *only* by conquering the *people* of the South, not just their armies, could the war be won. That is, even today a pretty ruthless doctrine of war. That it was meted out in full measure to those they considered their own citizens, will be fester in the collective conscience of the U.S for as long as it exists. Add to that the genocide of the so called Indians, whom we all now recognise as true Native Americans and we reveal a record on human rights which has its high points certainly, but its low points are very low indeed.

In the end the United States which finally matured and grew was Lincoln's vision and his achievement. This vision served as a beacon to oppressed and fettered peoples from all over Europe and beyond who came over decades, sailing past the Statue of Liberty to begin a new life of much greater freedom than any they had known before. But founded on four important wars, the first against us, the second against Mexico, the third against itself and the fourth the frightful genocide of the so called Indians, America has remained more willing than most western nations, who have gradually grown sceptical of the practicality of war, to project and sometimes use force to advance its interests, which it views as wholly beneficial to everyone.

The election of Barak Obama as the first black President has been universally acclaimed. He is, surely, the true successor to Abraham Lincoln and the symbol that the Union is at last of people as well as institutions. It has given the world hope that America has gained the courage of its original convictions and is ready to renew itself in a more inclusive mould, where consensus is seen as a virtue, not a vice, and the art of making friends is valued above the bombast of provoking enemies. As the nation closer to it than all others, we can help in this process.

But we will do so best if we cease to be the organ grinder's monkey and step out to make music of our own.

11

That music must be not the harsh clarion of the barrel organ, but the softer and more persuasive tone of the flute. The melody must soothe and inspire. Diplomacy must enjoy a renaissance; alliances must be made in the common interest, not in support of unyielding dogma. Enemies must become friends. British statecraft is arguably the best in the world with the longest unbroken tradition. It is now time for us to use it our way. If the U.S sees its interests differently, we should not fear to go where our own best interests lead.

Just as Lincoln arrived at the pivotal moment in America's history and laid the foundation of its superpower status, Obama arrives at a critical hour. For America has reached its peak as a world mega power and its influence will from now on decline. The shattering of its own financial model by its own prolificacy has dealt a fatal blow to the '*know best*' status upon which it has based its claim to strut so confidently across the world. Whatever it does from now on, it will never be taken as seriously again. It will be seen as it is, not as it says that it is.

We, in these islands are not strangers to these problems. We came through the Second World War victorious, but found our world influence diminished. We were seen as being on the decline, forever strapped for cash and yesterday's power. Our Empire grew restive. Parts of it rebelled. We learned to live, and then work, with terrorists, who became partners, often friends. The Mau Mau in Kenya, Eoka in Cyprus, the IRA; we treated with them all and brought them into government. Our Empire became the Commonwealth, which for all its faults remains a remarkable grouping for the common good.

For too long perhaps our politicians and mandarins saw the task as managing decline, but later this became something different. The word I think is renewal. We turned away from the nostalgia for our lost Empire and got on with life in the here and now. This experience will now help us help America. Although our country is tiny and America is vast, neither has a dominant tribe. Our people come from the Romans, the Angles, the Saxons, the Picts, the Jutes, the Celts, the Vikings, the Normans, and many others. More recently immigration from the Commonwealth and very recently Eastern Europe has added to the breadth of our cultural base. We have never fully repelled invaders; rather we have mostly absorbed them. America too has a great mix in the origins of its people.

We do have a difference in outlook. We see opportunities in international relationships and are good at finding common interest. We recognise that this may not mean common purpose, similar government or even shared values. But we do see everybody as part of the same human family. Too many American leaders see terrorists and rogue states, where perhaps they should accept people who are different.

There is a view already brewing among neo conservative Americans who have twigged that they have shot their bolt, that without the US as the global arbiter of who is acceptable and who is a rogue, the world is going to descend into a black hole of revolution and nuclear anarchy. In fact the majority of the people on the planet think the world will be a better, calmer, fairer place.

There is mounting evidence that the new President is more than sensitive to much or all of these things. He knows he must prevail over the political establishment at all levels of government and opposition in Washington. This will require leadership of the quality of his hero Abraham

Lincoln, by whose writings he was inspired during his long campaign to become the first President who is not white. The world is rooting for him.

We all need to remember that it was the U.S who gave us the internet, Google and Microsoft, the ipod and the telephone, put a man on the moon, came to Europe's rescue and spilt its blood in two world wars, saved Europe from starvation in 1945 and then gave the aid to rebuild its shattered nations, the list goes on. Always willing to make any sacrifice in the cause of freedom, listen to any idea from an innovative mind, receive the oppressed and the persecuted, America is there as a friend with opportunity in hope and with comfort in trial. There are few nations in history able to offer such a catalogue of achievement.

This does not mean that America is always right, or that in its attic there are no skeletons. We have considered a few; people will also recall the irrational paranoia of McCarthyism and the dreadful cost of the misguided strategy in Vietnam.

Neither does it mean that the United Kingdom cannot assert herself as an independent power. The three areas where a divergence from the U.S path is required are

Palestine, Russia and Iran. Set these three relationships on a more constructive footing and much else will follow. Let us begin with Russia.

12

Russia is our natural ally. We fought on the same side in the Napoleonic wars and in WW1 and WW2. It occupies the eastern boundary of Europe as we do the western. Europe is spread between us. Neither of us likes to become quite as involved in European affairs as the countries on the continent between us and we each harbour a fierce streak of individuality and independence. Both of us will compromise in the common interest. We in Britain have never been comfortable with whatever style of government Russia uses, but we recognise that Russians prefer strong leadership, verging on the authoritarian, rather than the adversarial democracy we favour.

We have leaders. Russia prefers a leader. We value opposition as highly as government. Russians do not. When we say freedom we think of freedom of speech and freedom of movement. When Russians say freedom they think of security from invasion, a steady job, enough to eat, public order, reliable basic services. These differences are not our concern. So long as we do not threaten each other's vital interests, how we live in our own countries is a matter for our own people.

We should take encouragement from the fact that Russia is now more democratic than it has ever been in its history and whilst the level of democracy falls short of what we regard as ideal, it is probably just about right for most Russians. We need to remember they have only been doing this for less than a score of years. We have been developing our institutions over many centuries.

When the financial structure of the rigid Soviet model imploded leading to the collapse of the Soviet Union itself, the West had a golden opportunity to extend a magnanimous hand and draw the new Russia into the European family by giving it all the aid we could to rebuild its institutions and its economy. Although we did extend a hand it was quite limp and the aid we gave was limited and heavy with conditions. The terrible lessons of the unfair treatment of Germany after WW1, lead to a much more enlightened approach at the end of WW2, when it was guilty of so much more. This leaves no excuse for the mistakes made in the 1990's towards Russia.

The Russians being a stoic people, put up with the West's self righteous admonitions, preoccupied as they were struggling for the basics of life, but they remembered their history and knew their day would dawn. If we had left it there and got on with our day, things might have worked out better. The problem was NATO.

NATO was formed in 1949 to counter the perceived threat of an invasion of Western Europe by the Soviet Union. For the first time it gave the US a permanent place in Europe as its leading military power. Following the decision to re-arm West Germany in 1954 the Soviets created the Warsaw Pact with all its east European satellite states as members. These two vast military structures faced in each other with frontline forces, missiles, sea and air power on station and at battle readiness for the remainder of the cold war without either firing a shot at the other. This must mark as history's greatest triumph of reason over bravado.

The Warsaw Pact was dissolved in 1991, when, with the collapse of the Soviet Union, the other signatories, none of whom were volunteers, walked out. It might have seemed logical for NATO also to be wound down. Two factors prevented this. One was a feeling that it was vital for the continent's future that the US remained an active player in Europe. We promoted that idea vigorously, as it always enhances our perception of our influence if the US is on hand. The second was that the US saw itself as the victor, as if the cold war had been a hot one, and now wanted the be the arbiter of a new world order. Keeping NATO intact would provide the means to give it a legitimate place in Europe.

It might have been more reasonable for the US to return behind its borders, as Russia had done. A European defence pact based on the European Union might have seemed logical. Britain and France with their substantial nuclear striking power could have provided Europe's nuclear umbrella for deterrence. But Saddam Hussein invaded Kuwait. The Balkans, in the form of Yugoslavia, fell apart. The resulting military emergencies provided a good reason to keep NATO going. Russia coped well with what might have seemed potentially alarming developments; until NATO began to expand eastwards into what had previously been the countries of the Warsaw Pact.

To understand Russian anxiety let us suppose it was America's financial system that had imploded (this may now seem rather near to unpleasant truths), NATO had been wound up and the Warsaw pact had advanced steadily west, welcomed by one European country after another. Would not the destitute Americans have felt threatened? Suppose Canada started to talk of joining the Warsaw Pact.

What would the neo-cons, albeit somewhat threadbare, have had to say about that?

It gets more complicated. Countries like Ukraine and Georgia have a history of independence but also of attachment to Russia. Both were republics of the USSR. Stalin was a Georgian. Khrushchev was Ukrainian. They have large Russian populations. After the Soviet collapse they declared neutrality. Now NATO, driven by the Americans and the old Warsaw Pact states which have already joined up, flirts with both. Indeed the flirting was understood by the Georgians to mean rather more than that and lead them to launch a reckless attack on South Ossetia.

The Russians hit back with surgical skill and destroyed the Georgian military. The West claimed Russia was the aggressor, when this was plainly not the case. Relations have deteriorated. Russia claims to feel threatened by this relentless advance of the most powerful military grouping in the world. This group says it threatens no one. Russia says 'then why does it advance?'

To rub salt in Russia's hurt the US, with the subtlety of an overzealous chef who cannot restrain his use of the salt mill, firms up on its plan to site missiles in Poland, allegedly to defend everyone against a nuclear attack from rogue nations. The Russians get angry and announce counter measures. The world begins to wonder about the US argument for this provocative move and with good reason.

It is not possible to provide a reliable defence against nuclear attack. The essence of nuclear armament is that it changes the rules of war. The concept is called deterrence. If a rogue state decided what fun it would be to launch a few missiles at the US and Europe one morning after breakfast, that state and its entire population would cease to exist by tea time. Such is the retaliatory power of the nuclear armed countries that it makes war between them or against them on any strategic scale impossible.

It is difficult to grasp the scale of aberration in the Pentagon, if this fundamental truth is not understood. It means the new generation of planners has completely failed to grasp how it was that the confrontation of the cold war was sustained for forty years without the outbreak of a hot war. This business about rogue missiles is the same misleading analysis as the weapons of mass destruction in Iraq. The path to an escalating confrontation is beginning to look a little too accessible.

Into this delicate situation we now need to step with a completely fresh approach. It will represent a seismic shift in direction and a quite different philosophical basis. The first thing to understand is that Russia is a European power and working with her, without tension, is vital to Europe's strategic interests. This is more important to Europe in the long term than relations with the US. Russia has huge natural resources of coal, gas, oil and minerals upon which Europe will become increasingly and unavoidably dependent. There is no longer any credible military situation in which the many countries of west and east Europe should need to fight each other.

The goal must be to bring Russia into Europe as a full partner of the European Union and a member of NATO, which should be reconstituted as a pan Europe alliance. America would remain a member but as time and confidence advanced it would need to contribute less and less. A Europe with the UK on the Western boundary and Russia on the east becomes the most significant grouping in the world, with a vast economy, enormous resources, industrial capacity and technology in all the branches of human progress.

Moreover the economic opportunities for modernising Russia's infrastructure will compensate in part for our dependence on their energy supplies. The integration of their military will provide a framework in which all the military elements on the continent of Europe can operate cohesively with each other as allies rather than in opposition. Europe will then have a united response to the issues of former Soviet states with large Russian populations and all states will be secure from within and protected from without.

With the ending of the cold war we reached a point in European history exactly similar to the end of WW2. With the fall of Nazi Germany we responded by bringing Germany in the European fold as a lead player with untold benefit to all. We now need the courage to see that the way forward is to do likewise with Russia. This is the moment for Great Britain to take the lead.

There will be much to do. Discussions with Russia will be quite demanding. It is no use using the sterile confrontational diplomacy that has us arriving with clothes pegs on our noses and a list of smells they have to get rid of before we can talk. It is now time for grown ups to take over. We need to find all the things we agree on and all the

89

common interests we have. That will show us both what we have to gain and will to motivate us to compromise on the contentious issues. It will all take time, but the very fact it is happening will send a signal into every hearth from one end of Europe to the other that times are changing and for the better.

We shall need to invest much time and sympathy with the State department in Washington and will need to select an Ambassador equal to the task. Looked upon objectively, America is in serious financial trouble with its major banks and corporations being baled out, part nationalised or both, all on borrowed money, most of which, we can see from the first chapter of this little book, will be coming from what was until recently the communist block. The US is approaching the point where it should welcome a reduction in the cost of its armed forces.

It is not necessary for America to be significantly involved in Europe militarily, if it can be assured that the new grouping does not represent a threat, which is why our leadership of the project is critical. America should not any longer cast itself as the world's policeman. Times have changed. The election of Barak Obama was universally welcomed because the world is no longer willing to treat with the old America. That is the major political reality the State Department is now facing. America has been saying for years Europe must take a bigger share of its defence burden. This new approach meets that criterion in a bold and imaginative way.

We must not expect the Americans to welcome the plan and initially we shall have to work hard with America as well as Russia, but we are more than equal to the task. In the end it will be for the members of the European Union and NATO to determine the outcome of any deal, but whatever happens we will have established a more constructive relationship between Russia and the UK which will be good for the two us as well as everybody else. This does not mean that we do not value as highly as ever the ties we have with the United States, nor does it mean that our admiration for that country and its people is at all diminished. It does mean that we will not pay the price of balancing all that by devaluing our potential relationships elsewhere.

Now let us turn to the plight of the Palestinians.

13

Readers will be familiar with the founding of the Jewish state of Israel in 1948, following the ending of the British Mandate for the territory known as Palestine. Although the Israelis accepted the partition of the area into two states the Arab negotiators did not and this led to immediate war. The following year a truce was signed but issues remained unresolved especially what to do about Arab refugees who had fled their homes in what was now Israel.

A further war erupted in 1967 in which the Arabs suffered a severe military defeat and Israel annexed more territory. In 1973 the Arabs, lead by Egypt, launched a surprise attack and Israel, at first hard pressed, held them off. In 1978, through the relentless determination of President Carter, accords were signed between Israel and Egypt that led to a peace treaty between the two and normalisation of relations. Other initiatives have followed, but with little lasting effect, though the dynamics of the tensions have altered.

First, the relationship between Israel and its Arab neighbours is no longer belligerent and no one realistically expects a war between them of any significance. Following Egypt's peace with Israel, Iraq sought to become the leader of Arab opposition and even attacked Israel with inaccurate conventionally armed Scud missiles in the first gulf war in 1990. Since the fall of Saddam, Iran becomes the main source of support for military irregulars, either terrorists or freedom fighters, depending on which side you favour.

Next, the actual issue that causes all the bloodshed in the area and which exercises almost all the political and diplomatic effort, is the plight of the Palestinian refugees, holed up in a self governing territory on Israel's western border, under siege most of the time by Israel and the source of intermittent terrorist attacks of various kinds upon the Jewish State.

There is a proliferation of Road Maps and Peace Plans which get nowhere, Peace Envoys from everywhere and dismay across the world that so many co-inhabitors of the old Palestine remain stateless and mostly dwelling in camps, sixty years on from the partition of the ancient lands of great significance to all three biblical religions, Judaism, Christianity and Islam. Moreover it is this festering sore at the heart of the cultural cradle of civilisations increasingly interdependent, which is the finest motivator for the young idealist to become attracted to the lure of terrorist sacrifice in the cause of fundamentalism.

Finally, the dynamic of the earlier wars was the support by the Warsaw Pact powers of the Arabs, which included comprehensive military equipment and advice as well as volunteers and advisers during actual fighting. The United States was, and remains, Israel's staunch ally and provided anything the Israeli's needed to establish the most formidable fighting machine in the region. There was therefore the restraining element of the cold war and a coherent and united position for both sides. After the peace treaty of 1979, the unity of the Arab softened and the Warsaw Pact gradually withdrew until the collapse of the Soviet Union ended its existence.

The outcome is that the US still backs Israel to the hilt and always will. The rest of NATO, whilst backing Israel's right to existence, tries to be neutral in matters of detail and hopes fervently that some durable and peaceful solution can be found. Meanwhile acts of terrorism killing the innocent, most of whom have no connection with the problem whatever, occur with distressing regularity right across the world.

There is now a certain lack of balance, in that whilst the huge weight of the United States tilts for Israel with a strange impotence at solution, no power speaks for the Palestinians specifically, though various Arab and European blocks and groupings declare sympathy.

A new US President with a less confrontational diplomatic model has made this issue a major priority. Faced with the worst financial and foreign policy failures of any incoming President in US history, this has been an early priority and the initial effort is very promising.

However, the region needs another active voice. Someone has to speak for the Palestinians, advocate their case, help them to construct a proper state and protect them from the bullying of which the Israelis have from time to time been guilty, most recently in their excessive attack on Hamas in Gaza. There is at the moment a dangerous vacuum here. The United Kingdom should step in to fill it.

It was after all the ending of our Mandate that marked the beginning of this terrible saga of violence and suffering. The good thing is that the Jewish people have been able to construct a viable and successful democratic state. The price for them has been the absence of real peace in their region and the sacrifice over the years of so many young lives. Israel must now recognise that after sixty years of intermittent war, there is no military solution available to them.

The bad thing is that the other half of the problem, the Palestinian refugees, almost all Arabs from that part of Palestine which is now Israel, remain stateless and deprived of civilised amenities as well as human dignity. For the most part they live in abject poverty.

It seems to me that we have a moral duty now to return to help these people to reach better times. Not more envoys and road maps, but expertise and financial aid to build an economy and a champion in the conference chamber. But not, if we have learned our lessons, troops, because that turns needed aid into unwanted occupation.

We have extensive experience of helping nations to independence and probably the best record in the world of bringing terrorist groups into mainstream government. We must talk to Hamas. If we threw our weight behind the building of the Palestinian state it would give hope and dignity to these deprived people, but at the same time give confidence to Israel and its ally the US that we would provide institutions and security to conclude meaningful negotiations and a lasting peace.

Of course we would not concede unreasonable demands from either side and we would be driven by the legitimate rights of the Palestinians, but this would not mean we are anti Israel.

On the contrary a lasting peace would be the greatest prize to which Israel can aspire. We have to agree an agenda with the Palestinians and then articulate their case. We must then make it abundantly plain to Israel the price it must pay for a lasting peace in terms of recognising the rights and aspirations of its neighbours, who must recognise the legitimacy of Israel in return.

14

Let us turn to Iran. I will be blunt. The West's stance in respect of Iran's potential nuclear weapons programme is unrealistic. Like fire, nuclear weapons exist. We helped invent them. America is the only country to have used them and then against an enemy who could not retaliate in kind.

What nuclear weapons have done is to prevent a third and even perhaps a fourth world war. They have saved the lives of countless millions. We cannot afford to get rid of them until there are universal institutions and a general agreement that major war is no longer an option open to humanity to resolve its differences. The good thing is that in my lifetime thus far we are further along the road to that prospect than at any time in human history. Unfortunately we can easily drive off the road because we do not realise where we are going.

At the moment nuclear weapons are held in readiness by America, the UK, France, Russia, China, Israel, India, Pakistan, and North Korea. South Africa has rid itself of them and Libya has halted its programme to acquire them. In reality it makes no difference to everyone else whether Iran is added to the list. They cannot use them against

Israel because Israel would retaliate in kind and the US would obliterate Iran anyway. What nuclear weapons do is to provide for nations which have them security from nuclear attack by others. If I were an Iranian I would look at a nuclear Israel and its mega power ally and I would wonder. This is not to say I would need to, but we must accept that it is understandable that I would worry.

It is too late now to generally isolate and antagonise Iran with sanctions and inspections, because there is no reason, if countries in its region like India, Pakistan and Israel have the deterrent capability, why it should go without. Of course it would be very much better if it did not feel the need. Isolating Iran will heighten its desire for the protection and status of its own weapons. If we talk to them, without preconditions and recognising their right to nuclear armament, we may stand a better chance of persuading them.

Resolving the inflammatory situation in what was once Palestine so that Arab and Jew can live in harmony with peace with justice for both, will be a huge step on the road towards getting to the level of international trust and mutual interdependence throughout the world, which will make the abolition of everyone's nuclear weapons a more

99

realistic prospect. That is the goal at which we should aim. What a supreme prize in the evolution of human history awaits us if we score.

It is that prize which should be the target of every young idealist of every religious faith, not carnage in the marketplace through the explosion of the suicide bomb. We can never win a war on terror. We can launch a serious drive to remove the causes of frustration that drive young people to terror. The real war worth fighting is against war itself. We need all the allies we can get in that campaign. Even Iran.

15

Of course, there are others issues in the world which almost daily bring a headline, but in a single part of this little book, I have concentrated where we need to reappraise and reassert. There are some points worth making in conclusion.

It is a fact that you cannot liberate a nation from itself. Do not be fooled into supposing that invading another country will free a people from a government we do not like. In the end all governments, even horror regimes like the Nazis, function only because the population acquiesces. Only when the people rise does true liberation come. This is why the Soviet block collapsed. It began with an exodus of Trabants from East Germany. But it succeeded because it was the people across the region who wanted change, not because a conquering army drove in out of the dawn.

The handling of the issue of Iraq will be judged the greatest foreign policy disaster of the post cold war period and certainly as far as the UK is concerned since Suez. We all know the reasons why. Yet had the West been more savvy after recapturing Kuwait, not imposed sanctions on Saddam, made sure that aid was given to repair vital services damaged in the war, made sure that the lives of ordinary people were normalised and especially that sick children did not die from medical embargoes, the Iraqi people themselves would eventually have changed their government, or their government, previously an ally of the west, would have become more liberal. By invading we toppled Saddam, but the consequently suffering of the Iraqi people has been appalling.

Likewise, Afghanistan. We should have known from history that this is an unconquerable land. We had the recent experience of the Russians with over a hundred thousand troops in the country and still they could not win. Here we are, eight years on, the Taliban growing steadily stronger with no end in sight. As we see, the terrorist camps have moved to Pakistan. Wherever you chase terrorists they will melt away and regroup. Of course we want to see a modern, secure and free society in that country. To the extent that this is possible the only route is economic development, deep in and long term. Any improvement achieved by an increase in the military effort is likely to melt away when the troops withdraw. This is what happened to the Russians. It may even happen in Iraq.

Both these wars were launched under U.S leadership in response to 9/11. This was the response to that astonishing blow to American prestige and the shocking loss of completely innocent life of ordinary people. It was the wrong response. Revenge is rarely a good counsellor. What was needed then was a steady nerve and a mature assessment of why and by whom and with what objective. America was unlucky to the extent that it had as a government the least well suited political grouping that it was possible for fate to assemble. These people went right back to the reaction to Custer's Last Stand. The Indians are the baddies. They committed an outrage. We are blameless. We have a duty to avenge our innocent heroes. People cannot do this to Americans and get away with it. We are going to hit these people hard and drive out the problem, once and for all.

This was what Al -Qaeda hoped they would do. 9/11 was a trap. Now, eight years on, we have a ruined Iraq slowly clawing its way back to stability with an uncertain path ahead, a destabilised Pakistan, Afghanistan in turmoil with the Taliban resurgent, North Korea assertive and nuclear armed, Iran determined to join the club, a huge erosion of personal freedom in the US, U.K and Europe as a consequence of the ill conceived war on terror, with terrorist threat levels remaining at an historic high. Now the military objectives are becoming confused. Strategists begin to talk of wars that can be lost, but cannot be won. Those are fundamentally the wrong sort of wars in which to become engaged.

In both these wars, after years of effort with thin if any reward, the doleful lament to our fallen young, who sacrifice themselves for us in those dusty fields, goes on. We have managed to get out, nearly, from Iraq, largely because the Americans have been willing to take over our watch. From Afghanistan there is no clear exit. To remain will be to lose many more valuable young lives and to what end?

There is literally no end in sight. We must not get embroiled in such muddled agendas again. We have to get a grip of our independence and start to think for ourselves. Nation building is difficult at the best of times, but impossible with an occupying army, however its presence is dressed up. You can only succeed that way if you conquer first, as we did Germany after world war two, or the Union after it conquered the Confederacy. Nobody has ever conquered Afghanistan. An army of over a million troops would be needed to do that and impose a proper government afterwards and fortunately there is no chance of such a force being assembled.

To build this nation into something approaching a modern state will require someone to come up with a completely different plan. Terrorism has many roots and to the extent that this is one of them is because we sowed the seed. The stark simplicity is that all these troubles have at their heart the failure to bring peace between Israel and the Palestinians. We need to bring all our limited resources to bear on that issue, since in its solution and its solution alone, sits the key to the solution of everything else.

Generally our approach to foreign policy needs more to recognise that different countries and cultures will not always function according to our western ideals. We need to be more respectful of those with whom we differ, whilst standing firm in the defence of our own values. We also need to be more astute at weighing the delicate balance between stability and ideal government. People may suffer under an autocratic regime, but in a destabilised and chaotic country or region, their suffering is all the greater. Above all we must learn that in the modern world the time has passed when we can sent in troops and impose our will. We really do have to face reality and move on.

We must embrace a new strategic focus to inform future foreign policy. The areas of the world where destabilisation poses the greatest risk to everyone else are undoubtedly Afghanistan, Pakistan and India. There is no solution, only exacerbation, offered by military intervention. To neutralise this potential flashpoint we must achieve a settlement in the Middle East, bring Russia into NATO and build on the current positive relations with China, while leaving the Chinese and Taiwanese to draw closer together in their own time. As a bulwark against the spread of fundamentalist revolution Russia and China are Europe's natural allies.

America, sometimes described as 'Europe Overseas', is family. There is a difference.

Blueprint

1 **To develop an independent foreign policy based on a British view of the world**, recognising that this may differ in emphasis and substance from that of the United States.

2 **To work to bring Russia into Europe as a full member of both the EU and NATO**

3 **To take a leading role promoting Palestinian interests** to energise meaningful progress to peace in the Middle East through the building of a viable Palestinian state which can be trusted by its regional neighbours.

4 **To cultivate a much closer understanding with Iran based upon a realistic appraisal of its rights as an independent country** which it must balance with international obligations. This will not be achieved by setting pre-determined agendas and pre-conditions.

5 **To build on good relations with China.** China will eventually become the single most powerful nation on earth, economically, militarily and scientifically.

6 **The Global Financial Crisis has increased cooperation between countries with different social and ideological cultures**. We need to extend this new reality with positive diplomatic initiatives.

2010
A Blueprint for Change
Part 3
Chapters 16-24

The Constitution

In recent times events have occurred which have brought the integrity of Government and more recently Parliament, into disrepute. The invasion of Iraq with its infamous dossier, the complete failure of Whitehall with its army of experts, regulators and quangos to see the banking collapse coming and the ghastly business of expenses have combined with other smaller irritants to shake everyone's confidence in our democratic system. Government appears to have been focussed on its interests rather than ours. Moreover it increasingly tells us what to do, when in a proper democracy the reverse should be the case. The time for some adjustment appears to have come.

16

Our constitution has developed over centuries and must be the longest unbroken state structure in the democratic world. It is unwritten and continuously evolving through practice, statute and precedent. The most recent significant changes came with the devolution of Scotland and Wales and the partial reform of the House of Lords.

Constitutional crises are rare because of the flexibility of interpretation. There are many checks and balances and much of the fabric is based on compromise. Like the original US constitution which fudged the issue of State sovereignty, we too had issues relating to the power of the Crown versus that of Parliament, which also led to Civil War. We tried a Republic, but in the end preferred the Monarchy and restored it. Charles II was given back the power of his beheaded father but ever increasing power has been ceded by the Crown to Parliament.

The difference with America was that we did not have a written constitution, the quarrel was about the relationship of Crown to Parliament and how we wished to be governed. It was not about one region of the country seeking independence from the other. In the end we went back to our old way of gradual constitutional development. This has over the ensuing centuries led to the transfer of all actual power to Parliament, whilst leaving all notional power with the Crown.

A good example to illustrate the step by step nature of this shift in recent times has been the power of the Queen to send for an MP of her choice to ask him (or her) to form a government and become Prime Minister. The Queen took advice making her choice after her current prime minister resigned, as her father had done before her when he sent for Churchill while preferring Halifax, and always sent for the person whom the majority party advised would gain parliamentary support. But it was seen to be within the Royal Prerogative for her to decide.

She did this three times. No doubt on sound advice she sent for Eden after Churchill. When Eden resigned she sent for Macmillan, rather than Butler, whom many supported. When Macmillan went not only was Butler in the frame, but several other contenders, but she astounded everybody but the outgoing Prime Minister who had advised it, and sent for the Earl of Home, who was the fourteenth earl and not even a member of the commons. He did resign his peerage and managed to win a bye-election made possible by the resignation of the elderly incumbent, but it was an astonishing process even then. After that the arrangement changed. To avoid controversy the governing party would fist elect a new leader whom the Queen would then summon.

In my life seven serving prime ministers have resigned. In the last three cases, Wilson, Thatcher and Blair the party elected a leader before the Queen made her choice of replacement. In two cases, Wilson and Thatcher, the election of their replacements was made by the governing parliamentary party. Since then all political parties have widened their electoral franchise to include subscribing party members. In the case of the Labour Party this includes block votes of trade unions.

This is where the Constitution might have become overstretched. Had someone opposed the elevation of Gordon Brown to the leadership of the Labour Party requiring a party ballot, the democratic thread would, in my view, have snapped and a constitutional issue would have arisen.

This is because in all the processes previously used for changing a prime minister, only elected members of parliament have been eligible to take part in the selection process if by formal ballot and by ministers, peers and the monarch if by discussion. All have been part of the structure of government. Party members and block votes of trade unions are not legitimate elements of this constitutional process.

We have never had a situation where members of one party outside parliament have been able to influence the monarch's choice of prime minister. For a party electing a leader in opposition this presents no problem, but it is undemocratic in government, unless the new prime ministers asks for dissolution and immediately goes to the country in a general election.

A solution would be to agree that when in government, only elected members of parliament can be involved in any ballot to choose a leader. Alternatively it could be accepted that immediately on appointment of a prime minister chosen by the monarch on the basis of an election process involving all party members, parliament would be dissolved and a general election held.

The counter argument against this analysis is that it is only the party leader who is being chosen by non members of

113

parliament. The serving prime minister does not resign until the new leader is elected. The Queen then sends for the leader of the majority party and all the constitutional niceties are met. Although this is true in fact it is not true in spirit as it would be perfectly clear that the new prime minister had been chosen with votes by the non parliamentary members of one party.

We need to accept that times may become less tolerant with long term effects of the recession and of global warming and political parties may become more polarised and to our eyes extreme. An ambiguous process might be dangerous. Remember Hitler came to power through a rickety democratic process, which he then abolished.

That example gives us due cause to consider some key aspects of our constitution and prompts some ideas for improvement.

17

There are four elements to our constitution; the Monarchy, Parliament, the Church of England and the Judiciary. Absolute power rests with the Monarch, but he or she can only exercise it through Parliament; the Judiciary is independent in its interpretation of the law of the land; the Church of England is part of the fabric of the State.

Since the Restoration in 1660, when absolute power was restored to the King, Parliament has gradually taken control of the exercise of that power to the point when today, all power is in the hands of parliament and none with the sovereign. Yet in one of those eccentric British compromises that makes Britain unique among democracies, although all government is in the *name* of the sovereign, it is only at the *will* of an elected parliament. It his Her Majesty's Government, Her Majesty's Armed Forces and so on. By modern convention the Prime Minister must be chosen from the House of Commons, rather than the Lords, though it is acceptable to have various members of the Government in the Lords.

My choice of words was careful. Chosen from the Commons, not by the Commons, although as we have already discussed, in practice it is the Commons which does the choosing. This is perhaps the most interesting subtly of our constitution. Put there to restrain the exercise of unreasonable power by the crown, parliament, to fulfil the need for ever greater democracy, has over the centuries taken more and more power to itself, to the point where today it exercises absolute power on its own. Yet it does not formalise the position, for fear I suspect the people might wake up to what has happened and say no.

They would not say no because they want an omnipotent king or queen, nor would they say no because they do not believe in their democracy. They would say no because on examining the matter, they would remember that in a democracy it is they, the people who are sovereign.

They might as the argument was explored discover that their parliament was not as efficient as they would like in fulfilling its democratic obligation to them. They might find that as taxpayers a great deal of their money was wasted, much of what they were told was not strictly true and that almost all government decisions were taken in secret, coming into the open only when a majority in the commons was a foregone conclusion.

Although there are from time to time exciting debates where sufficient government party members vote against their party to cause a government defeat, mostly the whips make sure members do as they are told. People often reflect among themselves that had the majority party been honest about what it was going to do if elected, they would never have voted for it.

Very little material is available to reveal the thinking process of government other than that which comes to light in leaks. Such leaks frequently reveal ministers to be, at best, opaque with the truth. The suspicion that stuff is happening and we are not being told, is well founded. Recently an M.P was arrested on some peculiar charge, the essence of which was that he had encouraged a civil servant whom he knew, to feed him leaks which would show the government was telling lies. Early morning raids on his home and offices by anti terrorist police (including his parliamentary office causing great controversy) were suggestive not of a democracy, but a most virulent dictatorship.

The Government first asserted that it did not know, next that it never interfered in police matters, then hinted that although matters of national security were not actually involved, they could be. This was unconvincing. Major leaks of national security do occur but investigations are carried out covertly and it is the job of the security services to deal with them. Of course there will be a few highly sensitive documents that are not security sensitive in the strictest sense, but these are as likely to be left on trains by civil servants as leaked to M.Ps.

The fact of the matter is clear. There is no greater threat to national security than a secretive and untruthful government. Against this eventuality we have no clear constitutional safeguards.

The culture of secrecy over quite trivial issues relating to the conduct of government business is all pervasive. There is confusion between what constitutes national security and what constitutes government embarrassment. Governments have assumed that they can tell the people one thing and each other something quite different and more recently have sought to brand those who feel it their duty as citizens to expose such duplicity as common criminals.

In the constitutional compromise, where formal power remains with the sovereign but actual power is entirely with parliament, another element in between is arguably the

118

most powerful. This is the Civil Service. At its local level in say a job centre, a civil servant who works helping people find employment, is exactly as the title suggests; an employee of the state working for the benefit of the community. At its most senior level, the knighted heads of the great Departments of State with their senior deputies, all highly educated with top degrees from the best universities, the civil service controls the levers of power.

It is their advice which guides ministers, their management which gives effect to policy, and their information which is fed to parliament in response to questions. These people are not really servants of the people. They are the masters. Yet in this open democracy they operate mostly in secret accountable only to each other. They work not for parliament but for the crown. Every resource they employ, whether it is the hundreds of billions of pounds spent by their programmes or the soap in their washrooms is provided by the citizens who pay the taxes, which are their inexhaustible cash flow.

This is does not mean that the civil service is in any way deficient or untrustworthy. It is perhaps the best public administration in the world. It keeps the wheels of our nation turning in peace and in war, whatever the government of the day. Yet in a modern democracy, so much of the working of our government is hidden from our view. This jars. Occasionally senior officials appear in front of parliamentary select committees, which do an excellent job ferreting out poor governance and financial prolificacy, but these excellent committees lack real power.

This has led to a whole industry devoted to leaks. It is considered part of the proper duty of opposition members of parliament to acquire information from anonymous sources which indicates that all it not exactly as ministers are saying. This has been going on for decades. Churchill harried the Chamberlain government with all kinds of information about growing German military power throughout the appeasement period, gaining wide popularity with the people and the displeasure not only of the appeasers, but also the King. Indeed without the groundswell of popular approval for his outspoken courage, it is unlikely he would have become prime minister. Had he not, there is little doubt that the King, Halifax and others would have made peace in 1940 or 1941 leaving the Nazis masters of Europe and the conquered peoples to their fate.

Leaks can change the course of history. Politicians of all shades have built their careers on them. They keep the
120

electors from being mislead. Yet should they be necessary? Ought not this major sector of government, responsible for implementing policy chosen through the democratic process, be more open?

The answer must surely be yes. It is true that the Freedom of Information Act makes it possible for us all to apply to see official documents and this is a great step forward. However it leaves the onus on the citizen to apply, which can only be done if the citizen knows what to ask for. The general culture of secrecy which pervades the system remains intact. This is what must change.

It should be a constitutional verity that paper, whether hard or electronic, produced by publicly paid persons using public money in its preparation is public property. From this starting point restrictions should be applied to protect state secrets, military plans and personal data and so on, but all other material not so classified should be free of restriction. Leaking it should not be a criminal offence.

In the event of a contentious leek, it would be for the government to prove beyond all doubt in Court that the leek damaged the interests of the State, rather than the interests of the government. In a modern, open, democracy, government must be transparent to the citizens who put it there and who pay its bills. We know who our elected representatives are and which of them form the Queen's government, but there is a lot else we do not know. We need to know more of the thinking behind its decisions, what advice it receives and from whom.

18

We need to redefine the relationship between the crown and parliament and crown and people. At present parliament places itself between the crown and the people. Although the crown owns the government, the civil service and the armed services, it has no say in the matter of what happens and why. We describe ourselves as having a constitutional monarchy. This is a very British fudge. Nobody knows exactly what that means, so there are no real checks upon its function. This is the more so since we do not have, in the formal sense, a constitution.

What we mean is that we have a ceremonial monarchy. The trouble is that this leaves all power with parliament in the absolute sense. In constitutional terms, parliament restrains and controls the government of the crown, which at first look offers the check and balance available in most republics between president and legislature. In fact is does nothing of the kind as the crown is now powerless, but in that curious British fondness for mystery in public affairs, so that we should not know that the crown is powerless, it is in the procedural sense all powerful. In this curious dance of constitutional veils between Her Majesty's Government and

Parliament, the people who pay for it all are allowed to play no part.

Their only say is through their votes at a general election. They have no say in when these should occur and there is no constitutional safeguard as to their regularity. In practice it is agreed that no parliament should last longer than five years. This is parliament's own arrangement which is free to break if it chooses. It did so in WW2. Parliament was elected in 1935 and should have gone to the country in 1940. In fact it decided to extend its term to the end of the war. Thus the same parliament sat without re-election for ten years. In the U.S., Lincoln had to seek re-election during the Civil War, Wilson during WW1 and Roosevelt in WW2.

This ability of parliament to essentially do anything it likes needs looking at. There were major questions of whether to make peace or continue with the war in 1940, about which the people were kept in the dark at the time and in the further dramas of 1941, remain in the dark still. It should have been possible to put such questions to the test, which is what a general election in 1940 would have done. There would have been the appeasers, by then a peace faction and there would have been a fight on faction, which would most likely have won. We were after all fighting a war to, among other things, preserve democracy. It is a rather defeatist admission to have a democracy that only works in peacetime. To happily suspend it in war suggests that it is not taken all that seriously.

An important element of our parliamentary structure is the House of Lords. When I was young it was entirely hereditary unless you became a bishop or a senior judge. It was in its day an enormously powerful assembly and was unusual in that both the Church of England and the Judiciary were represented, as well as the aristocracy and the nobility and, as we see from the ceremonial opening of parliament each year, the monarch has access.

During the twentieth century its decline in influence gathered pace as universal suffrage advanced. Acquiring peerages through wealth and later the introduction of life peers, has tended to reduce its aura and make it seem irrelevant. Recent scandals involving lobbying for fees has made it seem downright seedy. The whole appointment process of who to put there for life is so discredited as to be beyond public acceptability in a democracy. Ever since Labour came to government in 1997 there has been talk of reform, but so far all that has happened is that the hereditary peers have been reduced to under a hundred and the judges are being moved off to a new Supreme Court. Endless consultations, the holding bay of modern government, continue.

All of these observations lead to a single conclusion and a number of opportunities for reform. The single conclusion is that our democracy is a rather old an inefficient model and the time has come for a make over. As I write this chapter the expenses scandal is breaking, with daily revelations and a rising tide of public anger greater than I can ever recall. The time for change is ripe.

19

The first adjustment needs to be in the way the crown's absolute power is exercised by the monarch and by the monarch's government, which is provided by parliament. A lack of balance has occurred since all meaningful power is now taken by the prime minister, backed by a parliamentary majority. In a republic with a 'ceremonial' president, rather than an executive one, there are usually responsibilities to preside over the process of choosing a new government or dissolving the legislature for new elections. Unfortunately all of this is in the absolute control of our government without any check, except from parliament. Because of our party structure and the power of the whips, there is realistically no check at all unless there is major rebellion by members of the governing party or if there is either no majority or a very small one. Some of this power needs to be exercised again by the crown independently of parliament, specifically when to dissolve it.

The monarch should have an obligation to dissolve parliament and put the matter to the people if a government becomes so fractured in its unity as to inhibit effective government in the national interest (John Major) or wishes to go to war on a false premise with widespread opposition (Tony Blair and Anthony Eden) or ignores a manifesto commitment on a major issue (promising a referendum on an EU Treaty).

Other circumstances could be agreed, though the list should not be long. At present the crown has the power but would not exercise for fear of causing a major constitutional clash with parliament. This is a serious weakness and leaves citizens without an ultimate champion of their liberty.

I have always been uncomfortable that something so fundamental and history changing as the Abdication in 1936 was never put to an electoral test. I am even more uncomfortable with the failure to have an election in 1940 and for the 1935 parliament to run as it did for ten years. As I have said elsewhere the Americans have to have elections in war time. Not only has it done them no harm, but it has rekindled their resolve. It really is absurd to claim a democracy when citizens have no say in issues which require them to lay down their lives.

Republicans will argue that we must not increase the power of the crown. I agree. This proposal does the opposite. The crown already has the power, but this proposal confers a statutory obligation to act to protect the interests of the citizens and give them their democratic right to decide when exceptional conditions unforeseen at the time of the original mandate arise. The principle that the crown has an obligation to preserve and safeguard liberty and democracy in a line direct to the people, to protect them from oppression by parliament, will be an important part of ensuring the monarchy remains the centre of national stability and has relevance beyond the ceremonial in the century to come.

We need to look too at the lifespan of a parliament. At the moment it is a maximum of five years. Mostly prime ministers ask the Queen to exercise her power to dissolve parliament after about four years, or if the majority is too small sooner. Occasionally a parliament runs its full term, or at least within a week or two. Sir Alec Douglas-Home went the full length in1964 and John Major did so in 1992 and again in 1997. The problem with this established prime ministerial power is that it gives the government the facility to call an election at a crafty moment when they spy an iceberg on the horizon, which cannot bee seen by the electorate. Alternatively they totter on when their authority is spent.

Allowing the serving Prime Minister to decide may result in a new mandate which would not have been given, if it had been known that his ship was on a course for disaster or an uncomfortable passage at best. This power can lead to spinning the electorate to vote for one thing but to get quite another. I would favour fixed four year parliaments which can only come to a premature end if the government is defeated on a vote of confidence or the crown exercises its statutory power under the proposals above. I also think it is time we required members to get there on a majority of the votes cast. For the commons I do not favour transferable votes. I prefer the top two candidates going forward for a run off one week later. This preserves strong government but on a clear mandate.

20

Now we must consider the structure of the House of Lords, but not for long as the solution is pretty obvious. A fully elected upper house is a pre-requisite of a modern democracy and ensures that power is defused and not too heavily concentrated. One third of the House of Lords elected every second year for a six year term, would give continuity as well as renewal. This would also introduce the process gradually as it would take six years to complete the first cycle.

There would be many options to consider regarding the voting system and the nature of the representation. My personal choice would be for a one hundred member chamber with constituencies of each county in the UK, plus major cities, not more than eight, including London, Edinburgh, Belfast, Cardiff, Manchester and Birmingham. Voting should be proportional for each candidate on the pattern of that for the London mayor. Candidates could be from any party or independent. Existing members, either life peers or hereditary, could offer themselves for election.

The reason I favour constituencies is that the present arrangement is unrepresentative, with ordinary people having little idea of who the lords are or why they are there. It is certainly the case that the standard of debate in the lords is usually high with arguments addressed in a way which members who need votes to get there might not be willing to risk. Such an argument leads to a preference for a proportional system based upon party lists.

The counter to this is that extremist parties gain access on a relatively trivial number of votes and then exercise undue influence. It is only partially democratic as voters have no say on the identity of the people they are electing. I believe strongly that we must have full democracy; free open and representative, for both houses of parliament and the advantages greatly outweigh the snags. We need to remember that the constitution has at its apex the crown and even with the statutory obligation to defend the democratic rights of the people which I propose, it is still based on the hereditary principle and is not democratic. The people of this country are for the moment happy with that, but it is, for its own defence, the limit of anything short of full democracy in the governmental structure.

I come now to something new which, though at first sight may seem irrelevant to some, in our modern multi-faith culture, could provide a most valuable focus for developing understanding and tolerance between members of our different religious communities. I will call it the House of Faith.

The idea would be that there should be a *third house associated with parliament*, but not directly part of the legislative process. Consisting of representatives from all the various strands of religious faith now active within our communities, it would provide a meeting point and a debating forum to examine social issues and offer leadership in their resolution. It would have the power to propose social legislation to parliament, though not the power to be engaged in the actual process of adoption to the point of it becoming law. This would continue to be the responsibility of the commons and the lords.

With the democratisation of the House of Lords, the Church of England bishops would presumably not have seats. This will raise issues concerning the establishment of the church and the role of the other churches. This proposal will not only provide the forum to engage all the faiths to find the common path upon which their communities can travel in harmony with each other, but will also enshrine in our constitution the right to hold faith. Parliament would have to approve the admission of any faith to this third

133

house, to safeguard it from penetration by extremist or malicious groupings with violence as their creed.

21

We now have to look at the emotive question of MP's Salaries and expenses. In looking at that we need to re-examine what their job is. There is a popular belief that the M.P's job is in London helping to run the country, or if in opposition to oppose the government party in the adversarial system to which we are wedded with such enthusiasm both in politics and in the practice of law. This is not really the case nor is it how the parliamentary system was designed to work originally.

The job of the MP is to look after the interests of their constituents and to represent their interests in parliament by holding the government, which is the Crown's, not Parliament's, to account. Their main work and their office should be in their constituency. They should come to Parliament when relevant debates and other business require their attendance and to vote on legislative issues. The job of the government is to govern, or better put, to ensure that the structures and workings of the state function efficiently at affordable cost for the public good and that those charged with delivering public services do so properly. It must report to parliament on its effort and seek parliament's approval for any new legislation and for its programme for taxation and expenditure.

It is neither the job of government nor of parliament to continuously enact new laws governing every aspect of daily life to the extent that there are so many laws and regulations subject to endless change that few of the citizens paying for all this have a clue. Moreover the incestuous and frenzied environment of what has become known as the Westminster Village diminishes the quality of both government and parliament to the point that nobody in it can see the wood for the trees.

The outcome is inappropriate wars, financial calamity and generations of indebtedness. The finger of blame is pointed this way and that, identifying only fools and knaves, because the real blame lies in the entire parliamentary process which has failed and let the people, who trusted in it, down on a greater scale than at any time in our history.

The remedies are simple. First cut the pay of MP's to £50,000 per year. Second, eliminate expenses apart from travel to Westminster or on other public business, with overnight accommodation when necessary at utility prices. Being a member of parliament is not, neither should it

136

become, a career. It is a public service. It is not a lifetime activity. Members should be restricted to a maximum of five terms.

To do it you must have gained respect because of achievement in your career thus far whether it is in business, trade unions, social work, the arts, sport or whatever. To quote Abraham Lincoln, democracy is government of the people, by the people, for the people. At present we have government of the people by professional politicians and too often in their own interests. Not only is this not democracy, it is very bad government, as the truly appalling results now show.

Arguments about second homes will stop because there will be none. MP's will be required to live in (not have a stop over in) their constituencies and will be disqualified from parliament if they don't. Their office and their staff will be in their constituency and paid for by the parliamentary authorities. No more family gravy trains.

Parliament will meet, except in emergency for not more than one hundred days in a year and when it does it will be focussed and effective. No more of these debates on obscure but far reaching issues with a tiny handful of members

137

present. No more speeches from the throne listing a bewildering array of new bills. We have problems because we have far too many laws. Government is not about legislating. It is about delivering.

For this reason the balance within parliament needs to reflect more accurately the fact of the Crown's government and the people's Parliament. This is not difficult. The introduction of Select Committees is the most positive element of parliamentary development post war by far. Their capacity to summon witnesses and their public questioning of top policemen, civil servants, bankers as well as ministers and others have become a very important part of the work at Westminster and shows modern parliament in its very best light.

Where they fail is that their reports, which frequently reflect a much more accurate and shrewd assessment of a problem or chain of events than that presented by the government, do not have any teeth. Their findings command widespread interest and respect, but the governments of the day can, and mostly do, ignore them. We could change this, so that a Select Committee's recommendation would become binding on the government. To maintain checks and balances the government could have the recommendation overturned by the House of Commons on a simple majority. Select Committees, like Government would sit throughout the year at times of their own choosing. Parliament would not have to be in session for their operation, but any dispute between an SC and the Government would require resolution by the House of Commons.

Those elected to Select Committees, which would be a parliamentary function and nothing to do with the government which would have no say in their composition or chairmanship, would receive an additional salary and allowances equivalent to a Junior Minister and the Chair would be paid the same as a cabinet minister, all calculated as additions to the basic of £50,000.

With a more democratic parliament and a more clearly defined functional relationship with the government, it would be beneficial to allow non members of either house to become ministers. The convention that ministers have to be M.Ps is a confusion of function which does not always provide the best people in government. It would be feasible to allow up to half the government to be this class of minister. They would be required to attend the commons and lords to present their policies and answer questions and could join in debates relating to their department. They would not, however, have a vote, so the essential balance of elected members of both houses would remain the same.

This already happens on a small scale with the appointment of life peers by the Prime Minister, who immediately join the government. That will no longer be possible with the reformed House of Lords. This new proposal will allow good people to be brought into government in a more open and acceptable way, but when they leave government it is over for them. This leads to the issue of Cabinet reshuffles, a completely ridiculous practice. It should be established that a minister who falls short leaves the government and he cannot be replaced with another minister during that parliamentary term. New blood would be required.

In the event that more than three ministers resign at once, the government itself should resign. This need not, under the new structure, require a general election, if the Crown could offer to Parliament another Prime Minister, who need not be a member of either House, whose proposals for government received a majority in a vote of confidence. It would not be in the power of the Prime Minister to ask for dissolution, nor would parliament be able to dissolve itself.

This power would be statutory, clearly defined and held by the Crown as Trustee for the people.

22

Next we need to spend a moment on the origins of legislation. Almost all of this presently comes from the government of the day. There is far too much of it. A great deal of it is irrelevant. The judges will tell you much of modern legislation in thoroughly badly drafted.

We need much less of it and it needs to come more from parliament and less from government. One third of legislative business time should be open to Member's bills. The Leader of the House of Commons, who is the parliamentary business manager, is presently appointed by the Prime Minister and is a member of the Cabinet. That should change so that the Leader is elected by Parliament and serves a twelve month term, which can be renewed each year, but only for the life of one parliament.

Good government comes from efficient management and leadership, not from an endless stream of legislation. Democracy is about the people having the power through their elected representatives to hold the government to account not just at elections, but whilst it governs. Notionally our system works like that. Unfortunately designed for private members upon whom the party whip has been grafted as an add-on, it has fallen into decay to the point where our governments now possess excessive power.

In redressing this and charting a new path for legislation as well as a new and better purpose for it, we need to remember devolution, local government and the EU all of whom have power and responsibility for the lives of our citizens. The more those citizens can exercise their democratic rights in a way which has relevance to them, the greater will be the health of our democracy and the better will be the people who they elect to serve them.

At the parliamentary level the people have lost respect for and confidence in their representatives almost entirely. At the local level they see their councils having less and less authority to take decisions. At the European level they look and wonder. Only in the devolved areas is there a feeling that maybe things are getting better, but even here only just.

23

We need to look at the Monarchy, as an institution. I have left this till last, because I wanted to deal with the central issues of reform within our parliamentary democracy first. The truth is, however, is that the monarchy is central to all of it. I have already suggested certain statutory functions being exercised by the crown in order to defend and protect the democratic and constitutional rights of the people. I think this principle should be extended to the crown itself.

In reaching this conclusion I have been much influenced by the constitutional scandal of the abdication. Because that is what it was. A hugely popular King who spoke his mind and made little secret of his lack of faith in the competence of the Establishment to cope with the scourge of unemployment and the threat to peace of a resurgent Germany, was a thorn in the side of the Baldwin government. Seeing in his unfortunate devotion to a twice divorced American of rather singular aspect and knowing the emotional sensitivity of the young man brought up in the worst strictures of German parental tradition, Baldwin saw a chink through which he could drive what amounted to a coup.

Following consultations with the Dominions which we now know were nothing like as unanimous in outcome as the Prime Minister falsely represented, the King was told that if he did not dump the love of his life, the Government would resign. Maybe a Stuart King would have told them to go. One feels a modern Tudor would have for sure. Churchill, alone stood with the King but he was out of office. When he brought the matter to the Commons, Churchill was humiliated by the members, probably on the only occasion in his unique parliamentary career. So the King went and Baldwin won. Importantly the crown was silenced and has remained silent to this day. It is a matter of fact that no ordinary person has a clue what the Queen thinks about anything to do with public policy, as this is the constitutional convention.

This is what is described as a constitutional monarchy. It is more precisely a ceremonial monarchy allowing *de facto* the prime Minister of the day to become Head of State. This arrangement greatly empowers the Establishment at the expense of the people. It also keeps the family Windsor in fear they might lose the Crown. If the British people decide they no longer want a monarchy, so they should. But this is not the fear which stalks the Royal corridors. It is the possibility that once again the government could act

145

unilaterally over the people's heads. The Queen has so conducted herself with discretion over nearly sixty years that, apart from a wobble over Diana's death, she has a record of service to her country unsurpassed by any of her predecessors and the thought of getting rid of her has not crossed the mind, even for a moment, of any of her governments.

With Charles on the throne, according to leaks as George VII, things might not run so smoothly. Having carved a unique role for himself in a complete working lifetime of waiting, he has not only become a very successful property developer and grocer, but he was almost the original environmental campaigner. It is doubtful that without the Prince of Wales there would be any organic food production beyond allotments and country gardens. Most of his pronouncements are in tune with the public mood, but more often than not disliked by the government and derided by the establishment, who see in him a champion to raise the awareness of the people to their covert failures.

The word is that when King he will have to shut up. Really? I wonder. It is surely unlikely that he will become barren of views other than those of his governments, nor that he will be willing thereafter to talk about paint brushes, whilst ignoring the picture. Especially so if he thinks it is a picture which is being concealed from his people.

A non executive president in a republic has certain reserve powers and protections. I have already talked about the powers which we should transfer from parliament back to the crown in the interests of protecting democracy. I think we need to add a protection for the crown itself. In future it should be impossible for either government or parliament to force an abdication without a single issue referendum. This would protect the crown from a political coup, but at the same time restrain a rampant monarch, who, where he or she to lose such a referendum would lose all. It would also further enhance the democratic control of the people, by the people for their country, to paraphrase Abraham Lincoln.

This all presumes that the people of the United Kingdom wish to remain so and not become the United Republic or even a collection of separate republics. Making the assumption that the monarchy remains the popular choice is I think valid at this moment, but may not endure forever. I think it will endure for longer if it has attached to it statutory functions, obligations and protections similar to a non executive presidency. People will see a purpose in which they can take pride and a protection from which they can take comfort. This will be important whilst parliamentary institutions are rebuilt to a robust and democratic proficiency rather than the dysfunctional shambles which too much of them have become.

If in the end Republican sentiment rises to the point of challenge, the constitutional modernisation I propose would allow for the replacement of the crown by an elected president without much further adjustment.

24

Clearly the changes I propose should not all happen at once. It is certainly the case that some are needed now. I hope that the ideas outlined above will set people thinking, to bring public engagement in an important debate about the future structure of our democratic tradition. There is evidence of the last thirty years that professional politicians and a professional parliament are bad for democracy and produce bad government. Civil Servants are the professionals, Ministers are those responsible for policy determined by a mandate from the people and parliament is the people, by representation, holding the government to account.

Parliament must become more representative and made up of people who are something other than politicians and whose experience brings wisdom and independence to the House of Commons. Under no circumstances should they be in it for the money, or regard it as a way of life. They must not have their snouts in the trough, nor get any expenses other than reimbursement for basic travel and overnight at a tourist level hotel or parliamentary hostel when parliament is sitting. Expenses incurred on parliamentary business should be paid by the authorities direct.

Nobody will do it, will be the cry. The best people will go somewhere else. Rubbish. At the moment we have the worst, some of the very worst. The best people are not in politics, they stand disgusted on the sidelines. Make no mistake they will come forward and will be happy to represent their neighbours and serve their country for the perfectly respectable reward of £50,000 a year. The discovery of what MPs have been up to with their expenses, especially those who are well off anyway, is the greatest single shock to our democratic fabric since the days of Oliver Cromwell.

Its impact could be just as far reaching.

Blueprint

1 **The balance of power between Crown, Parliament and People is disproportionately tipped towards H.M Government at the expense of the People.** The Crown must be given the statutory responsibility to protect the liberty of the people through maintaining effective parliamentary government with a clear mandate. The

Crown should be required to dissolve parliament and put the issues to the people in certain limited circumstances.

2 **Parliament should operate on a fixed four year term**, and only dissolved earlier if the Government is defeated on a vote of confidence, of if dissolved by the Crown under its statutory obligations above.

3 **The House of Commons must have members elected by a clear majority** in each constituency. The best option is a run-off of the top two candidates after one week.

4 **The House of Lords must become a fully elected chamber**. The recommendation is for one third of the House to be elected for a six year term every two years with a maximum period of individual service of three terms. The House should consist of 100 members, one for each county in the United Kingdom, including Northern Ireland and an additional eight representing London and seven other major cities.

5 **There should be a new House of Faith**, with leading figures of all the major religions in the UK as approved by parliament. This new institution would have the power to introduce to the Commons social legislation, but not to

approve it and bring it into law, which would remain subject to the current process.

6 **All information and minutes whether paper or electronic produced by the civil service through the use of public money shall be deemed public property** unless excluded on the grounds of national security or personal data. The government would, if challenged, have to prove in Court the validity of any such exclusion.

7 **The way MPs are paid, what they do, where they do it and with what powers needs significant reform to restore democratic legitimacy and balance.**

8 **Abdication should be by referendum only,** unless through infirmity or illness.

2010
A Blueprint for Change
Part 4
Chapters 25-30
Health

We cannot talk seriously about health in the UK without looking at the National Health Service. It is the centrepiece of our public institutions, held in great affection by the people and the iconic symbol of the post war social revolution. It is the foundation of the welfare state and no politician can speak objectively about it without risk of electoral defeat. It is the largest employer in Europe.

The concept that the State has and can discharge the responsibility of healthcare for its citizens without charge to them directly is as valid as the state providing the army or the fire brigade. Healthcare is not a business, nor is it a centre for profit. Public healthcare has no more right to deliver a service that falls short because it is free, than the armed services have the right to neglect their duty of protection on the grounds that they are not mercenaries.

However, the armed forces can only be as good as their equipment allows and if we do not spend enough on them we and they pay a price. The NHS costs about £100 billion a year currently. It is free and available to all, but all pay for it in taxes. The question is whether these huge resources deliver the best possible outcome. We also need to ask whether the way the NHS is organised delivers to patients who are paying for it a timely and user friendly service.

26

The NHS is generally regarded as the best health service in the world and to the extent that it is free to all and provides total cover for the whole of life, probably it is. Yet all is not right. There are periodic reforms which disrupt staff and cause controversy, which make little practical difference to patients. These reforms appear structured for statistical impact so as to reach some target or make some economy. Waiting lists are reduced, but there are still waiting lists. Emergencies still languish on trolleys in A&E, if not for quite so long. Expenditure rises yet we spend less on healthcare than many other countries.

If you take the sum of the extraordinary dedication of all its staff, add to that the immense accumulation of medical knowledge and skill, then infuse the vast logistical resource, capping that with the eye popping budget and set all of it against the outcome to patients, what do we find? We find an organisation capable of extraordinary feats of lifesaving care in time of crisis on the one hand and a lumbering, bureaucratic, inefficient and confused monolith on the other.

The NHS is world class in any emergency such as a terrorist attack or air disaster. Trauma care for any emergency dash to hospital is almost always world class. In preparations for any coming pandemic the UK is regarded as a world leader. For complex medicine such as transplant surgery there is real and outstanding expertise. Recently I read of a woman who suffered cardiac arrest while out, was given resuscitation by passers by and paramedics then airlifted to a major hospital for heart surgery so that she not only came back from the dead, but was back at work and leading a normal life three months later. It is perhaps no coincidence that in all these areas the plan has to put the patient first above everything, even the wellbeing of staff.

Unfortunately it is in the treatment of everyday conditions, illnesses and mishaps of the kind that any member of the community can suddenly encounter, when the delays, rigmarole, rules and inertia come to the fore to make, for many, being ill a quite unnecessary trauma. It is here that major intervention and reform is required. Practices that have realistically nothing to do with patient priority must be stamped out. Bureaucracy must be subject to a tsunami and the medical profession must come down off its high horse.

Over the decades one Health Secretary after another has come forward with improvements. Many of these have been cosmetic. Others are real but ineffective. A few have been fanciful. All the time demand grows. Yet never does the NHS deliver an outcome which satisfies overall. Maybe it cannot. Maybe the idea is too big. Maybe we will not face the bills, in the form of taxation, for the excellence which the NHS and its political masters declare to be there already but which the average patient with a mysterious ache and a fistful of negative tests knows is at best patchy and at worst a delusion.

At the heart of the NHS is the medical profession, without which it cannot exist. Here lies the bar to the aspiration which it, the politicians, the people and the patients aim toward but never reach. The archaic hierarchical structure of the medical profession and its unique relationship with the organisation upon which we all depend is a fundamental barrier to progress. This must change.

Before examining this issue which politicians fear to confront, it makes sense to look at what a first class health service should be expected to provide, not in the context of what the NHS habitually delivers, but what the specification for a decent service ought to be.

First it must be organised in a simple way with short lines of communication and the minimum of administrative cost. The bulk of all resources must be directed to treatment and not to bureaucracy. Although a national organisation, it must be subject to local political control in a similar way to education. It must provide round the clock cover for all the health needs of the population.

As a guide the common standard for responding to a patient in terms of lead times these should be

To see a GP   4 hours.

To see a hospital specialist on referral from GP   24 hours

To have surgery when diagnosed as needed   48 hours

To have scans, ultrasound investigations etc.   2 hours

To be treated as an emergency admission to A&E   5 minutes.

If a timed appointment is offered the waiting time should not exceed ten minutes.

In the context of current experience, except in acute trauma, these figures look impossible. There has, from the very beginning, been a culture of delay and waiting since the foundation of the NHS. It is an ingrained theme of the application of its skill, yet it is no more reasonable to wait for medical treatment than it is to be put on a waiting list for a fire engine. We have just become used to waiting. Waiting is a departmental industry of the NHS. What is needed, as with the fire department, is an organisation crafted to deliver an immediate response so that people receive the best modern treatment as soon as they need it. At £100 billion a year nothing less will do.

The NHS has always had to defer to the medical profession. Individually doctors are outstanding professionals dedicated to saving life and alleviating suffering, but as a professional group they are unable to deliver the knowledge and skill inherent in their calling in a way which is timely, patient friendly and cost effective, unless they do this for private patients. This is unacceptable.

Doctors are dedicated and devote their lives to helping the rest of us to get the best out of ours. The problem goes back to the beginning of the NHS. Instead of employing doctors directly in the same way as army personnel or the police, because of the natural desire of the medical profession to preserve its independence and not become smothered as another branch of the civil service, the doctors gave their services as self employed people under contract to the NHS and were paid fees in return.

In the relatively simple structure of the early NHS this worked quite well. We need to remind ourselves of the enormous leap in social improvement which the provision of universal medical care free and for all represented. The worry of how to pay for treatment among the less well off had been a social blight reaching back to the start of the industrial revolution and the attendant development of medical science. Small wonder that the mere fact of being able to have treatment overrode for the majority quibbles about waiting times and other peculiarities of management.

Starting as a child in a middle class home, typical of that period, where depleted private means spelt a modest but what one might call a genteel lifestyle, I can clearly remember the deterioration over the next twenty years in the aura which surrounded the need for medical help. What had previously been a courteous and user friendly health system where doctors, nurses and even specialists came to see you at home and treatment was promptly arranged, became a multiple, centralised, anonymous shuffling of masses of people to sit in endless waiting at group practices, hospital clinics and lists for surgery. It was free, so you must not grumble and moreover it was bad form to do so.

But people did. Governments proclaimed endless and mostly futile reforms, sensing restive voters who clutched at the NHS as a treasured icon, but wanted something more efficient and user friendly. None of the reforms have delivered what patients are looking for, although politicians talk excitedly on the media about the improvements they believe their policies have wrought.

This has lead to the establishment of a parallel health facility, based on insurance. It is now widespread, not only through private subscription, but also as part of employment packages like a pension and a car. If this were operating as a quite separate element in competition to the NHS, it would not matter. Indeed it would be a positive spur to standards. But it is only separate in part. Many of its doctors are also working in the NHS.

You may ask how this can happen. It happens because the taxpayers, through successive governments, allow it.

Attempts by brave politicians to stop it have met such virulent opposition from the doctors that the authorities always back down.

Let us look at the relationship between doctors and the NHS. It is not a normal one of employer to employee. There are two separate elements. General Practice, which is the official term for family doctors and Hospital Doctors, organised like the military into ranks House Officer, Senior House Officer, Registrar and, at the top of the tree, Consultant. In turn these are divided into departments relating to different aspects of the human body, where the ranking is repeated.

From the consumer's point of view how they are paid is irrelevant. What matters is how long it takes to get medical help at time of need, where this is provided and with what beneficial effect. Nevertheless there is a difference in the pay structure. GP's continue to be regarded as self employed and have a contract with the NHS to provide a variety of community medical services based mostly on the requirement of the patient, unless gravely ill, to visit the surgery for help. The financial rewards are excessive, paid by the patients in their taxes.

The hospital doctors are not as generously paid initially but when they reach consultant level they can take private patients after giving the basic time requirement of 44 hours a week to the NHS, by which, unlike the GPs they are directly employed. The odd thing in the hospital sector is not the excessive level of pay, but the incoherent way in which the doctors render service in return.

Instead of working some regular number of consecutive hours in shifts, which take account of the 24/7 nature of medical care, they work in blocks of four hours at a time. The requirement is for ten blocks of four hours in each seven days. Essentially this means that each consultant is contributing a fraction under a quarter of the cover required for one week day and night by a single doctor. Put the other way round on these minimum hours the hospital would require four consultants to guarantee that one was always available day or night, provided they work a forty two hour week. To manage on three a fifty six hour week would be required. With five consultants the hours would fall to just under thirty four hours.

Unfortunately the patchwork outcome of all these blocks of four hours arranged in a higgledy piggledy programme explains why people who spend time in hospital often find in the course of a week they are examined by a different consultant every day. Moreover, consultants have other duties connected with teaching, training and management, all of which are part of the four hour blocks. The most absurd arrangement is that once they have completed their forty basic hours, if they add a further four, they can then go off and do private work for significant additional rewards. It must be said that many recoil from this and give any extra time they can to the NHS, but there are others and there are a good many, who earn very significant sums form private practice, regarding the NHS as a sort of basic pay with the bonuses coming from private medicine. This has to stop.

That this presents medical cover lacking in cohesion is not surprising. I can state without equivocation, based of twelve years experience of caring for the complex medical needs of my own daughter, *that such a system cannot deliver timely, efficient, cost effective and patient friendly medical care.* The system is standing on its head. The patients have to adjust to suit it, when it should be designed to suit them.

If you have any doubts about it go, if you can find the money, to a private hospital. Medical knowledge does not vary between the private and public sector and remains essentially the same. What is different is that people pay to be treated in an environment where their wellbeing is given priority over everything else. In order to deliver the private health sector has to operate a massively simpler, leaner and more cost effective system. There is no reason why ordinary people who have already paid for their NHS in various forms of taxation which many are hard pressed to afford, should, just because they do not get a bill at the end of the session, have to put up with something less comforting or effective than the private patient.

27

The entire structure on which the NHS is based is flawed and however many reorganisations and reforms it goes through it will never work as it should. Bit by bit it needs to be closed down and replaced with something entirely different. In setting out a programme so revolutionary that reading more may prove a fatal experience to those wedded to ways of old, I must advise you that you continue at your own risk. I can assure worried readers that my proposals do not involve any form of privatisation, by the front or back door; quite the reverse.

At present the first port of call is the GP. They are invested in the public psyche and by official propaganda with wisdoms that they may possess but do not practice. They are massively overpaid and little they offer could not be provided by a properly trained prescribing nurse.

Once you get to see one, which is often easier said than done and done only in hours convenient for them, you are allocated ten minutes during which diagnosis will be conditional upon your problem being some obvious condition you could look up on the internet. The result will be a prescription for a drug or a declaration that you are suffering from a virus. Anything else will require tests, but anything beyond blood and excretory tests will require you to be referred on to hospital, where delay is the nectar of the process to which you are now in thrall.

That this kind of medicine is worth over a hundred thousand a year in pay and so precious that it cannot be practiced after hours or at weekends is an arrangement so peculiar that it shows a strange disregard for need from those who provide it to the beleaguered patients, who, to add insult to injury are paying by taxation, mostly out of much smaller incomes, for this inadequacy of medical care. The greatest irony of all is that the general practitioner is the most competent of all the doctors and has the power to do the greatest good.

Either the GP service needs to be abolished with nurses and pharmacists taking over, with the doctors drafted into hospitals on a military style call up to treat the needy and end the queues, or the primary care programme needs to be changed to do a proper job. Do not be fooled by the need for specialisation.

A doctor, trained for seven years free of charge at public expense is a doctor. They can gain experience certainly

167

through a lifetime of work, but unless they become surgeons, where specialisation of what amount to biological engineering skills is both necessary and natural, the custom of specialist physicians is simply a medical trade union practice of demarcation lines so as to add value and divide up the spoils. The rigmarole of the patient being shuffled from one to another, as can happen easily with one who is suffering from several infirmities is both demeaning for the sufferer and extravagant on the public purse. It is also a major source of delay.

Medical scientists will need to specialise, as will surgeons but physicians treating patients daily should not. This is because the body does not function as several unrelated departments. It functions as an interrelated whole. I know this because for eleven years I gave twenty four hour care to my youngest daughter who suffered from a rare congenital condition which no doctor in the UK had experience of or knew how to treat. The effect of the condition struck at almost all her vital organs and treating one with the specialist knowledge of the relevant medical luminary led invariably to problems in another. Over those many years, which exceeded the training time for a doctor, I had to learn, as did she, how we could help one part just enough to manage, without erupting a crisis in another.

At no point was I able to talk to one consultant with a coherent overview of everything. In the end it was this lack of a single medical expert that cost my daughter her life. She would be alive today if we had been allowed to carry on in the way we had previously managed, but the system would not allow that. I was not recognised by the system as having any medical competence whatever and those who were recognised were too specialised to provide the balance of care and treatment upon which her life depended.

For me and for my family this was a tragedy from which we will never fully recover. For the NHS this was a wake up call to the dysfunctional nature of its core medical structure which not only costs lives, but hoovers up resources. It is just not possible to deliver coherent and cost effective medical care by such a fragmented approach. It works very well if your problem fits the system, or because of the scale of the emergency, the system becomes more flexible. This is at the heart of the matter. At its root the NHS is a system. It needs to become a facility. To do that, doctors will have to change their ways.

Do not be fooled either by cries that all the doctors will leave the NHS and go into private practice. Let them. Call their bluff. Remember the miners, British Leyland and the riots in Wapping. In the end there are more decent fair minded people and that includes doctors, who will step forward to a higher calling when the moment for change arrives.

The truth of the matter is that the vast majority of doctors are dedicated, motivated and selfless in doing their utmost to fulfil their calling and bring their knowledge to the aid of human suffering. Unfortunately they operate within an NHS which is so badly arranged that it prevents their full potential being realised. They are not blameless in this. Collectively the Royal Colleges and the British Medical Association have pressed restrictive practices upon the authorities for decades, although they would never admit to this. Individually many doctors are uncomfortable with the way things have turned out.

My proposals are radical because they are built upon patient need and require the organisation to form itself in shapes which will suit the community. The National Health Service should remain as an umbrella organisation, but operationally split into three components.

1 The Community Health Service.

2 The General Hospital Service

3 The Advanced Medical Service.

All Trusts and other quango style methods of management would be abolished.

28

Let us begin with the **Community Health Service.** This should consist of what we now call GP's supported by nurses, midwives, physiotherapists and pharmacists and any other relevant medical ancillaries.

It should have at its core a *medical centre* which in addition to routine consultations, would have the capacity to carry out simple x-rays, physiotherapy, ultra sound scans, all blood tests and other tests not requiring highly specialised equipment. It should also be able to deal with minor injuries involving less serious accidents but including simple fractures.

Another key component would be a *Community Nursing Hospital.* Here patients would go to be nursed and cared for when they were either too ill to remain at home, or there was insufficient care available for them there, or where more complex medication required continuous medical supervision. Like the old cottage hospitals, the doctor in charge would be the patient's own doctor.

GP'S would become *Personal Doctors* and the current practice of seeing almost all their patients in a surgery would cease. The PD would always visit patients at their home or in the local Nursing Hospital. The PD would own the patient and only in an off duty emergency would another PD attend. Doctors in present general practice have a wide and deep medical capability across the physical spectrum and across the age range. The present primary, secondary and tertiary system of care is wasteful, expensive, ineffective and anti- patient.

Doctors would be on 24/7 call with a rota to ensure time off and holidays, but nothing like the present arrangements of working four days a week and only in office hours. This is how it used to be and we have to go back there. It is the nature of the job.

For routine simple ailments, tests and injections, patients whose problem was not sufficient to prevent them going about their normal business, would visit the *medical centre* to be seen by a *Prescribing Nurse.* The PN would deal with the matter, but if necessary send the patient home to be seen as soon as practical (always that day) by the patient's PD.

There is a weakness at all the lower levels of current healthcare which must be addressed. This is diagnosis. The

173

order of training of the modern doctor is *first test then diagnoses then treat*. This works if the test is reliable. There are many conditions were either there are no tests or the outcome is uncertain. Patients suffering from one of these will have experienced a long and frustrating haul before the answer is found.

I have talked to doctors about this and they acknowledge that the modern approach which is very drug centred, does not always equip them with the same skills of intuitive diagnosis possessed by experienced family doctors of my childhood. There have been great medical advances in this period, but not always in the everyday treatment, to put us back on form when things go a little bit wrong.

As part of the local health facility and working as an integral element of the team there would be new rank of *Community Diagnostician*. They would be senior and experienced physicians who would provide a second opinion for Personal Doctors faced with a perplexing array of symptoms. Based at the Community Medical Centre they would normally visit patients with the PD at home, but they would have additional responsibilities to oversee the testing and investigative facilities at the CMC. They would not run clinics. There would be no clinics. These are time consuming, expensive and demeaning for patients. They do not exist in private medical care because organising them would be far too expensive and patients would not put up with it.

The combination of a Nursing Hospital (able to carry out minor surgical procedures and normal childbirth), a Medical Centre dealing with all routine health requirements and an organization of medical staff led by doctors providing homecare would thus provide the complete health cover that the vast majority of the population need in their daily lives.

The management would consist of a Community Medical Officer, a fully qualified, but not practicing, doctor and a Community Nursing Officer. These two key health leaders would be responsible for the proper distribution of resources and the maintenance of standards in medical care. They would like everyone else in the structure, including doctors, be employed by the District Health Authority. This would be organised on a similar basis to the current Local Education Authority and be part of the County, City or Metropolitan Authority, subject to democratic control with a Cabinet Member for Health as the political head.

Funding would be by central government based on population headcount augmented by other social factors and would be paid to the DHA. The DHA would decide on the distribution, subject to certain statutory requirements, and would be accountable to voters for the wisdom and effectiveness of their choices. The role of central government would be to determine, through the umbrella NHS overall health policy and provide the funding out of taxation, but it would not be allowed to interfere with local decisions.

The role of non- medically qualified managers and administrators would be hugely reduced and their numbers cut by at least two thirds, possibly even three quarters. At present there are more administrators than consultants and their numbers are growing. With shorter lines of communication, immediate response capability, resourced from the community in which it operates and shaped for local need, the **Community Health Service** would provide patients with an accessible, reliable and timely health facility quite different level to the present effort at a significantly lower cost. Further economic benefit would accrue from a gradual improvement in the overall health and wellbeing of the population.

In the contentious matter of pay, the general principle would be that we have allowed earnings to come out of balance so that the present GP's earn too much and the other medical staff, nurses, midwives, physiotherapists etc earn too little. This imbalance would have to be redressed. Greedy doctors would be replaced, although whatever the agitation at the time, they would be few in number. The vast majority of doctors are very decent people with a vocational calling who want to earn a fair living but are not in medicine for the money. Those who are must go and plough their own furrow.

4

Let us move on to the next segment of the reform to health care. The old Primary, Secondary and Tertiary levels of seniority within the bloated NHS, creaking under the weight of restrictive medical practices, waiting lists and bureaucracy would go and good riddance.

Most health maintenance and repair would take place at or close to home in the Community Health Service described above. More serious cases requiring moderate or major surgery or more complex diagnostic or treatment facilities than available locally, would transfer to the **General Hospital Service.**

This would consist of all the present district general hospitals and any regional hospitals which failed to meet the criteria for the final arm of the NHS described later. *GHS Hospitals* would be able to provide the full range of medical care, investigations scans and surgery which form the established level of medical and nursing practice short of the scientific cutting edge. The medical hierarchy would be new.

There would be no consultants and no physicians dealing with only one area of the human anatomy. As we have already seen, the present compartmentalised system contributes to cost and delay and is old fashioned, obsolete, inefficient medicine. Surgeons would continue to specialise when complex procedures were involved.

The medical lead in the GHS hospital would be the team of physicians, called *Hospital Doctors*. Each ward would have attached to it an HD who would take temporary ownership of the case from the Personal Doctor, while the patient was hospitalised. The HD would remain on the ward, there would be no clinics, rounds or meetings and they would be caring for their patients throughout the day. There would be no medical rank of registrar or house officer. Instead there would be *Assistant HD's* and *Deputy HD's*. Each ward, depending on its size, would have a team sharing three eight hour shifts, but not all would need to be on duty together.

It is impossible to overstate the need for physicians at this level to be competent in the diagnosis and treatment in all parts of the human anatomy. It is increasingly clear to all but the blinkered that good health depends on a holistic approach to lifestyle, diet, medical care and treatment. When the latter two are required the doctor must understand the whole of the patient, not just specialist parts, and organise therapy with due regard to the effect of drugs and treatment on unaffected elements of that patient's body.

Furthermore doctors should understand diet and prescribe it as part of treatment. For a doctor not to understand diet is as ridiculous as a pilot not understanding gravity. Moreover the unfortunate practice of passing the patient to a separate dietician, who lacks full medical training, is a silly has handing the aeroplane over to a gravity expert who does not know how to fly. There will be a lot more doctors needed as resources are deflected from the ludicrous miasma of quangos and management now bleeding our healthcare system to anaemia, and talented medical ancillaries such as dieticians and senior nurses should be offered the opportunity to be trained as full physicians.

Surgeons are the engineers of human medicine and such is the science and complexity of modern surgical capability, specialisation is not only inevitable but necessary. There is still a need for general surgeons and every GHS hospital should have several. The doctor would always remain owner of the case and in charge of the patient's overall wellbeing and recovery. The surgeon would operate and advise on aftercare, working closely with the physician. It may well be practical for a team of specialist surgeons to support more than one hospital and they would provide cover as required. The patient would not normally be moved.

Hospital Doctors would have the rank and seniority of the current consultant, but would undertake only one job at a time. Normally they would be engaged in full time medicine, in charge of their ward. They would not in this case be engaged in either management or teaching and there would be no permission to carry out private practice. On this letter point, the cost to every taxpayer of the NHS is now such that everyone is fed up waiting on lists and in queues whilst some consultants are moonlighting up the road. If these consultants have time on their hands it should be used to reduce these lists.

HDs who wished to teach would apply for teaching appointments which would be fulltime. This would not preclude them from later returning to medicine. Likewise HDs wanting to manage could do so if required, but the job would be full time and they would not be involved with patients.

Doctors or surgeons at any level wishing to engage in private medicine would be free to do so, but would cease to be employed by the NHS. Insurance operating beside the NHS without restriction, calling upon the services of NHS doctors has the effect of creaming off some of the best and most patient friendly facilities for the benefit of the few at the expense of the many. There is no doubt that the manifest failures of the NHS to develop as a patient driven organisation has given impetus to this and it will be the object of the reforms to redress that imbalance.

In order to give the reforms the maximum chance of success and motivated by the huge benefit in quality of life and economic advantage of a free ultra efficient public health facility operating within communities in timely fashion, it is proposed that a levy of 33% be added to every medical insurance premium whether actual, or notional in the form of a free benefit of employment. This levy would pass automatically to the NHS to be spent on improving still further public healthcare. At present the NHS is subsidising private healthcare, by carrying the cost not only of training of doctors and other medical staff, but also the cost of the entire medical infrastructure, save for a few private hospitals. This clearly is inequitable and the levy would help to redress the balance. Ideally the point would be reached where insured private health care was seen to be unnecessary. At present many people in demanding jobs simply could not function without it.

The *General Hospital Service* would be part of the umbrella NHS, managed and organised on a Regional structure. The regions would comprise a group of counties or similar and contain about twenty General Hospitals. Each would be led by a Regional Medical Officer and other management, small in number, who would report to the Regional Health Authority. This would comprise representatives from elected councils from within the region, as well as experts from the medical and care services. The elected representatives would have a majority.

As a public service, funded by public money, management by quango or trust, foundation or whatever is too remote from democratic control. The performance of the health facility at all levels must be subject to the process of local democracy in a much more direct and obvious way than simply changing the national government.

One of the reasons so few people vote in local elections is the feeling that it makes no difference to their lives. Having a direct impact on the quality of healthcare is a sure way of cultivating attention and a more dynamic interaction between the people and their local leaders. It also wrests control from central government, which, as a later chapter will argue, is over large and over powerful and needs its wings severely clipped. The current state of our country, plunged into the greatest peacetime crisis for more than a century, demonstrates the ineffectual quality of both national politicians and senior mandarins in Whitehall. We need to wrest much of the control of our daily lives to familiar faces nearer home.

29

At the top of the new organisation under the umbrella of the NHS would be the **Advanced Medical Service.** Unlike the other two elements in the new organisation, where the tasks and responsibilities will be clearly defined, the AMS would be more flexible and open ended. It would have a purpose certainly. That would be to advance, harness and deliver the cutting edge of medical science in the most up to date and complex forms of diagnosis, treatment and surgery. Instead of comprising only elements of the NHS it would include contributions both financial and practical from the pharmaceutical industry, equipment industry as well as the universities and other research bodies.

Comprising very broadly the current major teaching and specialist hospitals it would be led by the *Faculty of Advanced Medicine*, which would have a status in medicine equivalent to the Monetary Policy Committee of the Bank of England, to the economy. It would be necessary for the leaders of medicine and surgery to design a workable structure with the government of the day, provided it did not allow restrictive professional practices to inform process or suffocating bureaucracy to stifle it.

The objective would be to lead the world in advanced medical care and scientific progress, offering exceptional career opportunity and status for the gifted not only in medicine and surgery but in nursing too. This would provide patients suffering from complex conditions with a more timely response of much higher quality and with greater prospects of outcome. No longer would the UK lag behind in league tables of which country it was best to have this or that disease. The huge talent of our medical service would be, for the first time, harnessed to give our people a standard of advanced healthcare matched by none and uniquely free to all.

When the original NHS was set up the organisation created was probably the best that could be achieved at the time. Since then there have been enormous changes. Many of these have done little more than cause upheaval with marginal impact at the point of delivery. Politicians and political doctors whose medalling has rarely been worthwhile, have proclaimed reform, improvement and advance, but little of this is evident to those who fall ill and need timely help with what are for the most part every day conditions. In some areas things are better, for instance cancer care, but many other countries are better still.

Yet it does not have to be like this, nor is it always. Our ambulance service is as good as can be found anywhere in the world. If there is a disaster such as a train wreck or terrorist attack the whole medical system swings into emergency mode putting the victims at the top of the agenda with all other process suspended and delivers rescue and treatment in often acutely hazardous and difficult conditions which will not be surpassed in any other country. We can do it. Yes we can.

But we cannot do it on a routine basis in the present organisation of the NHS and no amount of tinkering and fiddling will make any real difference. There is no doubt we have the talent and the dedication of what may very well be the best health professionals in the world. But they are fettered by chains of a completely deficient organisation, operating unsuitable practices which leave the patient, whatever the lip service and propaganda, at the bottom of the pecking order and at the end of the line.

The final defence of the present failure is cost. You cannot provide an infinite service on a finite resource. No, but you can provide a very good service from an affordable resource if you set about the right way.

30

There is, of course, more to health than the NHS. It is not my purpose to preach lifestyle, yet readers may want to know my views. It seems to me that there are certain verities. In coming to this conclusion I have been hugely influenced by caring for an impaired life over more than a decade, during which magical time I learned that theories were one thing but the facts were often quite another. We tend to take, if we are normally well, health for granted. Yet good health comes not by accident, but by design and most of the responsibility for the design is in our own hands.

The human body is a machine, a biological one, but like all machines it depends on fuel. Like most machines the type of fuel and its suitability will affect the performance. There is an old truth that says we are what we eat. Broadly that is true.

Where the human machine varies is that there are no two identical and even among types there are individual characteristics. Hence the fact that people look different, have unique fingerprints and so on, even if they are of the same family or nationality. It follows therefore that there can be quite wide variations in the detail of the best food for each of us, because no two of us will handle it in exactly the same way. Personal health will reflect that relationship between what you eat, who you are and what you do.

This will, of course be affected by the current state of your body and its age. We must remember that some bodies have a manufacturing fault, others a programming error, some have been attacked and temporarily damaged by an invasive force, such as a virus or infection. Many of these conditions can be repaired, some by the body alone, others by the body with help. There may be a need for re-engineering which we call surgery. It may be that we have to make do with things as they are. Eventually the body will finally wear out anyway, or it may be overwhelmed by disease or suffer an organic failure. The objective of a sensible approach to health should be to get the best out of what you have, rather than to abuse it with misuse, poor fuel or bad practice.

I have studied the endless diet programmes offered commercially, some of which made their originators rich and whilst most have some merit, prescription dieting to a pre-made programme is not, I think the answer, unless there is a directly related issue such as disease, intolerance or allergy. What is needed to be effective and lifelong is a personal approach.

188

Mostly bad diet means one or all of three things. Too much is eaten, unhealthy food makes up the majority of the intake or, because of sensitivities, the food does not work well for the individual. A preference for fast food or an undue reliance on pre-prepared and processed food is bound to cause trouble sooner or later. To control your own food intake and get the best results for your own body you need to be able to cook. This goes equally for men.

Food should be cooked from fresh ingredients and from the freezer cabinet only in emergency. Fresh does not mean organic if you find it that too expensive. There must be plenty of vegetables and a balance between fish and meat and between white and red meat, unless you are a vegetarian. Potatoes and bread yes, but not too much. Cake, biscuits and pies are always bad but nice, so be sensible. These are treats not for every day. Packet snacks and sweets are very bad indeed.

I find for myself that I do not do that well on wheat or dairy products. I am not formally allergic, but I have less energy, feel less fit and am more prone to dry skin in the winter. I do not wander anxiously around health food stores picking at this and that, but as a general rule I prefer rye bread, oatcakes, goat's milk yoghurt and cheese. I never use any animal fat of any sort in cooking, mostly only light olive oil, but I eat and enjoy meat with bits of fat attached. I think this is a taste acquired from being brought up in food rationing. I might add that since giving up taking certain prescription drugs on a programme lasting many years, I have found I tolerate better a wider selection of ingredients.

When out, I eat whatever I am given (even a burger), but if I can choose I like Italian best and go for light rather than rich or heavy dishes. If I put on weight just eating less is enough to return to normal. I am happy eating meat and fish but vegetables and fruit are a key part of my diet and are eaten every day. We brought up six children and followed a similar pattern with all of them. Now grown up they are all healthy eaters by choice, but they have never really known anything else. All can cook.

If one is not overweight it is so easy to criticise people who are. Yet it is astonishing just how many people are so much heavier than was the case forty years ago. Some people have health issues which cause them to be overweight no matter what. The majority are overweight for the simple reason they eat too much. It may be made worse by eating the wrong kind of food (which tends not to satisfy thus increasing hunger), but the simple truth is that whilst everyone needs a slightly different amount of food to stay trim, far too many eat far too much. If you want to get your waistline down, forget faddish diets and expensive lifestyle courses; just eat less and better.

Good health does also depend on taking exercise and modern lifestyle and working practices make that more difficult for a great many. Do not be fooled into the supposition that you can eat as much as you like and binge drink often but workouts in the gym will put it all right. They won't. It may mask the damage you are doing to yourself like papering over cracks, but it will not provide a long term answer.

Neither will jogging several miles a day. All of this is good but only if part of a general lifestyle which is healthy. A work out in the gym at lunchtime will never do you as much good as walking to work if you can, speed walking up the escalator and taking the stairs instead of the lift. If you work in a tower, de-lift four floors down and finish the climb on foot. Get outside at weekends and never buy the Sunday papers. Anyone who sits around reading all that stuff on their day off has lost the plot when it comes to good health!

In the end always remember you are who you are, with a unique worth as a precious human being. Fat or thin, healthy or frail, celebrity or unknown, in the great scheme of things the value of all is beyond calculation but the value of each is the same.

The Blueprint

1 There must be a complete rebuild to a different shape of NHS, centred on the needs of the patients and the communities in which they live and work.

2 The relationship between the Medical Profession and the NHS has to be radically altered.

3 The NHS should become the umbrella of three separate components of healthcare, the Community Health Service, The General Hospital Service, and the Advanced Medical Service.

4 The current medical structure needs drastic change, to bring it up to date with modern needs

5 **The NHS has become** a system. It should be a facility.

6 **The NHS is consuming too much feeding itself** at the expense of patient care. Bureaucracy, administration and management will have to be massively reduced, then empowered and given the job to do unfettered by excessive reliance on process, with l full responsibility for outcomes.

2010
A Blueprint for Change
Part 5
Chapters 31-37

Education

This chapter is not about private education, further education, colleges or universities. It is about the basic education essential to the maintenance of a civilised and prosperous society and provided free to everyone, paid for by taxpayers. This is the concern of the great majority of parents and the sole route to learning available to all but the privileged, to whom the private sector offers a viable choice. I dislike dogma in education as it mostly leads to centralisation and failed theories. I do confess to one personal ideal. I believe that state education should be the best available to anyone. In some outstandingly led state schools it is, but mostly it is not. We need to fix that.

31

I am not professionally engaged in education, but I do have a good practical experience of the education process in England which, excluding my own experience as a youngster, now spans over forty years, as this is the continuous period through which I have had at least one of my six children in full time education. During this time I have watched with ever increasing dismay continuous political interference, most of it harmful, in a learning tradition built over centuries. This perception has been heightened by two periods as a state school governor, once quite recently and once in the nineteen sixties. Further useful input came from a family member who was a distinguished head of a progressive independent school. My own six children have attended both state and private schools in roughly equal measure.

Attempts to engage education as a vehicle for social engineering have been ragged in outcome, often making an improvement here but creating a problem there. There is a good deal of confusion among professionals about the difference between social engineering and social advancement. The former should not be attempted anywhere and certainly never in education. The latter should be the objective of all enlightened public policy and of this education should be in the vanguard. This means social advancement of the whole of society as the collective nation, not just the advancement of individuals for their own exclusive benefit.

To judge the effect and effectiveness of education we must look at where the country is headed, the quality of life, the cohesion of communities, the efficiency of government, the strength of our institutions and the viability of our economy. Because it is these elements of nationhood which stand as markers of performance, not league tables, nor statistics and above all not grades. It is the purpose of education to equip the rising generation to carry forward the baton of human progress. This has to be based on a foundation of wisdom born of knowledge of what has gone before. It has to be inspired by the will to discover new knowledge, in order to advance the barrier of human achievement for the benefit of all.

To do this, it is obvious that students need to be taught and have time to explore literature, history, geography and all the human and pure sciences, as well as acquiring the basic skills of communication and interface in reading, maths, languages and information technology. All of this must be

197

experienced in an environment where relationships have collective value, there is an understanding of right and wrong, community is revered and the difference between selflessness and selfishness is clearly defined.

It is odd that in the period since the introduction of the Butler Education Act in 1944, which provided free education for all for the first time, two recurrent and to some extent opposing themes have driven political activists leading to continuous tinkering. In the fifties and early sixties a widespread anxiety developed about a single examination; the eleven plus. This was seen as unfair, as it determined whether a child from a poorer background received the educational opportunity to rise above circumstances and achieve social advancement through the more sophisticated education available at the grammar schools. The alternative provided by the secondary modern schools, though offering a very good practical grounding, lacked academic focus and any drive for results. Indeed the school leaving age was fourteen.

Hate of this exam led to the introduction of comprehensive education, the abolition of most, but not all grammar schools, leading in turn to the other theme. Equal educational opportunity required a universal measure to be able to judge who was bright and who was not. The cop out word *gifted* was coined to explain why the educational system still had to cope with the simple truth that some people are apparently brighter than others.

The universal measure turned out to be more exams, in the end so many and coming upon each other so thick and fast, that education became not the acquisition of knowledge to cultivate wisdom and purpose, but the training of exam skills to a curriculum set by politicians advised by misguided academics, with teachers marginalised and without heed paid to their input. The totem before which all were required to prostrate themselves was the mighty and all defining grade.

The meddlers had taken away marks, because the competitive nature of such information would, they asserted, inhibit the less gifted. It also became impossible to fail an exam since everyone would get some kind of grade even if deep in the unexplored reaches of the alphabet. This has led, as those with common sense would have advised if their opinions had not been excluded by the avalanche of political and academic claptrap, to our current situation where only two grades count; an A for second best and an A* for the top. Every thing else is an also ran with which those who get them have to make do. Those without meaningful grades or practical skills are at risk of sinking into the underclass of benefits, booze and petty crime.

This is an appalling and unforgivable waste of human talent, made worse by the outcome at the top, which on some measure is no better. The people of our country stare in bewilderment at bankers who cannot add up or assess risk, governments which blunder into reckless wars and a parliament which is institutionally dishonest. All of those professionals, as they like to call themselves, with a few exceptions, have the best educational qualifications, often from the very best universities which demand the highest grades. Yet in the end what do all of them really *know?* Whatever it is, it is clearly not enough, or perhaps better put, not enough understood. In the headlong dash for grades, bouncing from one examination to the next, there is no time to dwell, to ponder, to refine. Knowledge is good, but without *meaning*, it is barren.

We need to understand that education is not a race. It is a right of citizenship and its quality determines the worth of the nation. It is as morally bankrupt to cast aside young human beings because of a failure to respond to an educational pattern, as it would be to cast them aside because they are black or female or obese or whatever. To waste human beings is to squander the most precious of all resources and to suppose that the only fulfilment of life is to become a highly paid professional not only expands this class of person to the point where they are in vast excess, but it leaves uncounted the essential network of practical skills upon which the quality of civilised life in the modern world depends. Moreover if the level of educational qualification, based on grades almost exclusively, becomes the main arbiter of selection, the outcome will be an unbalanced society, top heavy and inefficient, with a mounting gap between top and bottom and a state sector bloated to bursting point.

It is alarming to discover that in the grade focussed arena into which we throw the young to joust for their (and our own) futures, fewer than half last year were able to achieve A-C passes to include English and Mathematics. This proposes that the majority of the population are failed educationally. This begs questions of the educational effort; it suggests that the way we pass judgement or assess ability is flawed. Are we assessing the capability of the bus driver on their ability to drive a train? What do these grades really *say* about the candidate's knowledge? Make no mistake the chase for grades is as damaging, if not more so to the really gifted, for they are required to become good at exams rather than wise thinkers.

This does not mean that the gifted should not be given the right path to excel, to be streamed and grouped where stimulus will come from their peers. It is not elitist to put them in schools like grammar schools or in streams that would swamp the less academic. We need their genius more now than ever before. But we also need those with practical gifts to become the getters and doers. The quality of all our lives depends on their contribution and we need to respect that.

It is no more rational to prefer those who have a gifted brain than it is to prefer those born to wealth and aristocracy. In a balanced society, all have value, each plays a part, none are excluded and everyone pulls together. This cannot be achieved by demanding uniformity. It is found only through the freedom of variety. Wisdom is not an exclusive quality. Christians will recall that Jesus was a carpenter.

We do need lawyers, consultants and bankers. We need doctors and architects and journalists. But we badly need engineers, scientists and technologists. We simply cannot manage without nurses, health workers, plumbers, train drivers, bus crews and builders; the list is almost endless. We need them all to have the same basic education, so that they understand their heritage, have the basic work and social skills, know the ways of the world and how to manage the challenges and opportunities of life. Most of all they need to see themselves and respect each other as vital members of that national team which combines to make our nation. Their integrated effort will increasingly determine the quality of life for all.

32

In our very British way we are muddling (and meddling) toward these lofty objectives now, but with patchy and haphazard results providing some truly damaging outcomes. We need to find a more reliable compass to chart a surer path. We especially need to trust the dedicated army of men and women who make up the teaching profession to deliver a safe arrival and lift from their shoulders the weight of this fantasy that Whitehall knows best.

But to begin, we need to explore two fundamental questions. What is intelligence? Why do some have more than others? The answer to the second question should come first. None has more than their neighbour. All are born with the same amount. All of it is there from birth.

Intelligence is a measure to explain something, like the soul or the spirit or self, which is there but hard to define. Unfortunately the measures developed favour one sort of intelligence, whilst neglecting another. The truth is that intelligence is so vast and multifaceted that it cannot be measured. We can only discover that someone is good at maths or music (in some astonishing cases without having been taught either) or whatever. We try to pretend that the ability to spot a sequence or pick the odd one out of a group of funny shapes tells us something with a wider meaning than the level of ability in that exercise, or lack of it, on display.

The difference between individuals comes not from the level of intelligence of each, but the way in which they use their brains, what parts they use and how well they do it. When we teach (or bring up) children, we are essentially training their brains to work in a particular way. Some brains seem almost programmed already along the path we lead them, whilst others struggle and fall at every obstacle. Yet to dismiss these young people as somehow less worthy or less able is to proclaim our own lack of understanding of the huge well of human genius. In a moment of national upheaval from whom do you get the pithiest analysis, a group of clever investment bankers or a group of villagers in the pub? To use devised means to show up one group as clever and another as fools is to proclaim oneself amongst them the biggest fool of all.

This does not mean there should be no testing, or that everything in education in flawed. Nor does it mean that, for the moment, all exams should disappear. There is so much that is good in our education family, which is rich in both talent and resources. The issues stem from the hobbling of all this dedication and skill with a seemingly endless flow of directives from above and the stricture of due process. Indeed education mirrors modern society.

Rather than talk of more reform, of which there has been a great deal in the last sixty odd years, we need to think of releasing the boundless talent of both teachers and the taught to foster the inherent genius of human endeavour, now more advanced, yet in many ways more suppressed, than in any previous age of man.

Before we explore how this might be achieved in present circumstances, it might be helpful to look ahead in our mind's eye and what a school of the future should look like, for which we probably have the required technology already. We can then, perhaps, come forward with adjustments to provide from present resources a more effective and happier result.

The school of the future would not have a class and teaching structure as we have today. Each student would have their own dedicated work station with PC and all the latest technological facilities. Teachers, of which there may be several working as a team in each class, would move from console to console helping and guiding the students with a reduction in telling time and an increase in showing time.

All work would be assessed as completed to form a portfolio of achievement which would eventually lead to graduation from the school at three levels, Graduation, With Merit and With Distinction. No set piece exams would be involved, though testing would be continuous. Graduations would occur at the end of primary and at the end of secondary education, which would be at sixteen.

The strengths of every student would be developed according to vocation and talent to provide, in addition, Final Diplomas in the practical requirements of earning a living or the academic subjects grouped into arts, science and environment. The aim would be for every student to finish basic education with an outcome of value amounting to at least a Graduation plus a Final Diploma pointing them in the direction where their contribution to society could best be channelled.

After age sixteen students who were not going straight into employment or training would move to Advanced Education, currently generally provided by secondary schools in Sixth Forms or by separate Sixth Form Colleges.

Structurally there would be no need to change this. The course would be less computer focussed with students given every opportunity to explore a subject or more than one, in depth. At the end of two years there would be a traditional written final exam, to add value to assessments made on work during the two years. A pass would entitle the student to use the suffix A.E. or A.E. Hons. This would stand for advanced education and would be awarded in classes the same as university degrees.

Unlike the present system of centralised examinations with a choice of examining boards, each educational establishment would issue its own Graduation or Advanced diplomas, but these would have to conform to a common standard. This would allow variation to provide for particular speciality or emphasis of different schools and colleges.

Overall the purpose of education would be very much more to harness the collective genius for the common good than to weed out the best from the worst, which whatever the official propaganda may say, has increasingly become the outcome of the way things are done now. It would nevertheless provide for a very much more fertile learning environment, more likely to engage the aspirations of students at all levels of the ability range.

It would recognise what I believe to be so true. Everyone is equally blessed with the same intelligence. The difference is the ability to unlock its power and use it in a productive and fulfilling way. For some this may mean to scale the heights of science or literature, but for others the provision of the basics of civilisation may be the choice. We need to understand we cannot have the one without the other. We must learn that together they present a balance in value.

This new approach would provide a much less stressful and professionally more rewarding career experience for teachers whose role would be significantly strengthened through enhanced responsibility and freedom from interference. This does not mean there would be no checks or inspections, or that standards would be allowed to drift, or that bizarre regimes would be allowed to take hold. There would be supervision and an operating framework, but all much less procedural than at present. At all times and at all levels, those in education (as in everything else) would be given and take responsibility, not follow process.

An important part of teaching is the ability to keep order in class. Without classroom discipline, learning stops. I have known good teachers who are bad at keeping order. It is a difficult skill to train. Teachers need stage presence. If they have this in the way a good actor commands the stage, they have very little trouble with pupil order. The most disciplined classes fall into line naturally and not because there is some iron fist prevailing. Yet it is a peculiar fact that a class which behaves impeccably for one teacher can become little better than a riot for another.

One reason for this is that, as in every profession, there are teachers who are poor at teaching. Children have an instinct for identifying the good from the poor teachers and begin to do so at a surprisingly early age. As they grow older they become much sharper at this judgement, which I have found is invariably sound. They will then take it out on the bad teacher, whom they will regard as little better than a figure of fun. Whilst these unfortunate, but generally no less dedicated, staff may be poor *classroom* teachers, some of them can be very good with small groups or one to one.

This leads me to feel that the number of poor teachers if that skill is included, is smaller than if it is not. Under the advances in the education structure which I have outlined above, I would advocate that class discipline were in the hands of specialist class leaders, who were good at organising and leading, good at crowd control if you like, so as to leave the teachers to concentrate on the critical task of unlocking the potential of all those young minds.

All of this is, of course a glimpse into the future. Whilst a vision of the future is an indispensable attribute of leadership and of making public policy, we are in the here and now and we must look and see what can be done with what we have.

33

There are several parts to the organisation of our schools. Let me deal first, briefly, with the independent sector. Originally mainly single sex preparatory and public schools, all boarding establishments with some local day pupils to keep up numbers; these have now been supplemented with a number of day only schools, some co-ed, which have proved popular with parents in the locality who are willing to make the financial sacrifice to give their children the best educational opportunity. Some of these schools are very good but others are a complete waste of money. All independent schools are to some extent immune from the flights of fancy which pass for educational policy in government, but not entirely so, nor as much as they would like to be.

I am not much concerned about the private sector. First because it has been established for centuries, developing organically, building its practices bit by bit to reflect the need and fashions of the day and second because it is available only to the fortunate few, whose parents can, in addition to paying the same taxes as everyone else, afford also to pay the significant cost of fees.

The state sector is for everyone and free to all who use it, though one of the greatest elements in public expenditure. It is here that I shall concentrate, because I believe that with the resources and talent within its vast organisation it has the power to deliver by far the best education of all. A really good education is the right of every young citizen, but we need to understand that only if they can see its value and relevance to their own future, will they themselves utilise its potential for their own benefit and for society as a whole.

Before the reforms of the nineteen eighties which sparked a process of tinkering followed by all governments since, the structure of state education was straightforward. Under local authority control, normally at county level or equivalent, the LEA was responsible for, managed and ran state funded schools and employed and appointed all the teachers. Locally power rested with the District Education Officer. He or she was the person to whom the community looked for educational management. Elected councillors bore the electoral cost for failure, or received the dividend for success. Now everything is centralised, with local tokenism, disguised under the mantra of parent power, one of the most deceptive arrangements organised by a string of deceptive and power obsessed governments.

If we come to Academies and Trust Schools in a moment we can deal first with local authority schools of all forms and age groups. These operate under the auspices of the LEA, which has a lot less power than was once the case. Before it raised the education budget from the local taxation, supplemented largely from the Treasury grants, but with the right to decide how the money should be spent locally according to need and community preference.

It employed and appointed all staff and head teachers. It acted when circumstances required to support and reorganise failing schools. It could support a small school in a rural area at the expense of urban schools if there was local demand and take whatever political consequences or dividends followed. Unfortunately not all local authorities did these things well and some did them very badly. The outcome has been to give excessive responsibility to governing bodies, take power to Whitehall, bypass the LEA and pay schools direct so much per pupil per annum and leave the LEA in an advisory or partnership no man's land which costs a lot but can do little. This is the worst arrangement of all.

Everything is wrapped in a suffocating programme of due process, good practice and absurd official policies, which

214

have to be written down, agreed by the governors and formalised. The first question in a calamity is 'was the school following its agreed policy?' in playground supervision or whatever. Teachers, governors, ancillary staff and local authority partners spend hours and hours on this stuff, which not only wastes time and money, but saps initiative and withers creativity. When the time comes to assess how well it is all going, the school is required to fill up, which takes management and teacher time in lavish amounts, wait for it, a *self evaluation form*.

This pervasive absurdity of modern government that filling up a form, pages and pages long, somehow sharpens perception, enhances understanding and unlocks hidden wisdom, is at the root of much that is wrong in our country today. It must be supposed that hitherto politicians have been too engaged viewing things from a political rather than a practical view, to stop and think. Had they done so, they would have realised that it is impossible to scale heights of educational excellence if you treat those dedicated teachers and managers charged with the task as imbeciles. Excellence in education will not be found in forms, practices, processes and policies. What are needed are creativity, dynamism, leadership, initiative and responsibility. There has to be variety, because young

215

people themselves vary in a thousand different ways. In pursuit of the goal of excellence freedom must be the spur.

There is now a widespread view that comprehensives have failed. I am not sure that is the right definition. What has failed is trying to introduce uniformity. There are some good comprehensives. All ability education, although challenging if standards are to rise up rather than be dumbed down, is a worthwhile goal. It best suits smaller catchments where there are not the pupil numbers to justify different types of school.

The mistake was to make the concept universal. Grammar schools are good as an option in large areas. Schools with an accent on what we call vocational skills, offering a high standard of practical and relevant education to those, the majority in fact, who would benefit from acquiring a basic standard of learning with important life skills, should exist and be valued just as highly as other schools following a more academic path.

We need both. At present the whole system leans towards academic achievement with fewer than half all students achieving the basic pass of 5 A-C including Maths and English, as we have already seen. This is more than

216

disappointing and condemns huge numbers to low achievement. It also acts as a brake upon the brighter students who do not achieve their full potential either. The biggest failure of the comprehensive idea is that the bad examples of it fail both the under achievers and the clever in equal measure.

Yet the theme that education is not a contest, but a practical and important programme to provide each student with the character, knowledge, skill, self worth and sense of community to enable each to add value to the sum of human achievement, is now more valid than ever. My contention is that this can never be done well in a society which is diverse both in culture and in aspiration, by a system which is uniform. Diversity offers a surer route to a better outcome.

In the nineteen fifties there were mainly three kinds of state secondary school; secondary moderns, grammar schools and technical colleges. All were single sex and there were separate schools in each location for boys and girls. Education was focussed and effective but the gap between the attainers in the grammar schools and the doers in the secondary moderns was too great. Additionally the grammars offered social mobility; a plumber's child could

217

become a doctor, whereas the perception was that in the secondary modern the plumber's child stayed a plumber. In a time when social engineering and class levelling were a big feature of government, this perception, though not always accurate, led to the movement to comprehensive schools.

Now most grammars have disappeared and all secondary moderns. The comprehensive has become the common model, but more recently new developments have begun to offer more diversity. Faith schools, Foundation Schools, Trust schools and Academies are beginning to offer some degree of variety, often producing enhanced results over the schools they replace. They generally enjoy greater freedom over setting their curriculum. Specifically they operate independently of the local authority. These developments should all be regarded as positive, but more time will be needed to judge the overall impact on standards of education generally.

My own view is that while these developments are moving in the right direction there is one major issue, in organisational terms, to be addressed. It is the excessive involvement and centralised control of Whitehall. The Local Education Authorities, whilst having innumerable responsibilities, have surprisingly little power.

My own experience relates to a County Council rather than a Metropolitan authority, though the principles are the same. The CC has a Leader who heads a Cabinet, all composed of elected councillors. Each cabinet member has a portfolio, of which Education is normally the biggest, though presently disguised under the folksy and ridiculous pseudonym of Children Schools and Families. This includes the social services and special needs support for young people, but the department is dominated by education. Always the biggest budget by far the department is responsible for running education locally on behalf of the government.

This is the nub. Little of the core decision process remains with the LEA. The Secretary of State is the real person in charge and retains control of even, in the national context, of trivial issues. At the other end of the scale much responsibility has been passed to school governors. Needless to say there is a significant and costly support system to train volunteers how to govern. They find that much of governing is about superintending practice, procedure and adherence to official policies. This leaves something of a vacuum in the event of difficulty, but also leaves the democratic control virtually sterile. Voters can decide who

219

their elected representatives should be on their local authority, but these people will have little power to affect education policy.

Voters will also elect their national government, but this involves issues way above local worries about individual schools. It was not always like this. At one time local authorities had a real say in the way education was organised in their area. We need to get back to that.

The attraction of Academy type schools is that they are freed from government interference, save for regular inspections, and these schools have an important part to play in a developed system which offers choice and variety. They are much nearer independent schools in the way they are governed and run. Parents and the community have little say in the way independent schools are run directly, but if they do not approve the school and do not support it, that school goes out of business. This now applies to all state schools, because they are funded directly by central government at so much per pupil per annum. If numbers fall the school goes into deficit and eventually closes. Some may argue that this is all the democracy you need.

I am not comfortable with that. There is an important role for proactive local authorities to provide an educational option which they control and which is subject, like other services directly controlled by such authorities, to democratic remit of local taxpayers and parents. LEA schools do provide an important educational provision, often when other options are unavailable, but these schools must, in my view fall under the complete control of the local authority with the power to open and shut, hire and fire, organise a curriculum that suits the needs and opportunities of the area and be subject to the judgement of the local electorate at the end of the day.

There must be a national framework for education and statutory inspections to maintain standards, but government should not decide in a free democracy what is taught in our schools any more than it decides on university courses or what we buy in our supermarkets. As much as possible of what goes on in education should be decided at local level. One of the reasons for the low turnouts at local elections is that so little is really at the remit of those elected. People feel there should be more to local democracy than potholes and parking fees. Education should be a major local programme as should health, as argued earlier.

34

I have said little so far about primary schools, not because they are less important, but because so much is currently focussed in public policy on secondary schools, their format and objectives. Primary school is where it all begins and where so many seeds of future difficulty are sown.

Generally primary schools enjoy a close, sometimes special relationship with the communities they serve. This is because their catchments are much smaller and local. Mostly they follow the same format, though there are LEA, church and faith models. The problems relate to what they teach and how they teach it. This is not because they are bad at their collective job. It is because they are directed what to teach and how to teach it by Whitehall and its quangos. It is here that re-inventors of the wheel proliferate in large numbers.

It will be tedious for us all to dissect their barmy ideas bit by bit. I propose instead to lay out the basis for a firm foundation in knowledge which is the purpose of primary education, upon which everything else in future has to be built. If this foundation is incomplete all further learning is handicapped, if not for the pure facts, certainly for the knowledge of context which give the facts meaning.

By the time children reach eleven years old they should be able to read. They should be able to write fair English, meaning in a way others can read it and understand its meaning, not in some prescriptive lettering style fiddling over loops and tails, nor stuffed with excessive use of adjectives to create a florid and vacuous style. They should be able to spell all the words they would be likely to use.

They should have basic mathematical skills. This means they should be able to add and subtract, divide and multiply very accurately with a calculator and sufficiently without, and adequately to get by in their heads. They must know all their tables as the basis of their maths, not learn them bit by bit over years. They should know how to devise basic decimal formulae i.e. five per cent of something is multiply by .05.

Basic science in the sense of electricity, the elements, climate and the environment should be explored with markers to cultivate interest. We need scientists. The two most important words in education are why and how. They lead you to when. They also awaken curiosity in the young mind and set it on the path of discovery.

In a modern world computer skills are everything and many children are way ahead of the current generation of teachers in the use of this technology. Unfortunately there are still families who cannot afford a home computer and their children need extra help. Teaching of IT skills needs to be organised into two sets at all primary schools, so that those who do not have use of a computer as part of daily life, can get extra help to bring them forward.

Geography is a subject, like history, that at this level is completely off the rails. It is one thing to explore the topography of a local village, but this should not be at the expense of not knowing whether the Falklands are off North Scotland, West Africa or South America. The world of the internet is small enough to fit into every living room in the country. It is important that all children know about, continents, countries and capitals. Later they will learn about cultures, customs and racial harmony, but with little meaning unless they have a vision of the world as a complex interrelated political structure full of independent and diverse countries. The must know the oceans, the seas and the mountain ranges too, because in the era of climate change all this is critical.

History does not mean looking at photographs of the local town in the nineteen twenties or studying the Victorians in depth. It means having an overview of the broad history of our country from the time the Romans left, all our Kings and Queens, the key wars and battles, the development of Parliament, the rise and fall of the British Empire and so on. It is also important to know about the Reformation, and the part that Rome played as a basis of our civilisation and the Industrial Revolution. Many will disagree with this. To them I say history is a chain of consequences, since nothing in human affairs happens without cause. If we do not know the chain of consequences which washed us to our present shore, we cannot safely plan our journey onward to the future. None of this needs to be known in depth to start with but the broad picture is an essential pillar of education and the heritage of all children which we have no right to deny them.

It is not right to continue with a situation in which when I asked a group of bright ten year olds which came first Agincourt or Waterloo, they had never heard of either. Nor is it right that the gifted daughter of a teacher friend having

225

gained admission to one of our top universities to read History, her best subject, had to stay up nights studying all the history she was expected to know which she had never been taught.

Religion has become a confused and confusing subject since it became customary to study it as a sort of amalgam of interesting cultures and beliefs held by different people both within our country and across the world. Study of the bible has been abandoned in favour of a more balanced view. Unfortunately this overlooks the plain fact that our entire national fabric, both constitution and culture, is based upon the stories and legends (or irrefutable truths depending on your level of faith) of both the Old and New Testament and their impact upon politics and government over two thousand years. Whilst continuing to ensure all children have an understanding of the principal religions of the world and are free to believe in any or none, it seems essential that what was once called Scripture, finds its way back as a core subject in primary education. Without the overview of that knowledge, little else makes sense.

This mix of subjects which I think forms the essential foundation for a lifetime of engagement in both learning, leadership and living life to the full benefit of both self and community may seem old fashioned. It is not. It is timeless. Together it creates for children, many, too many, of whom are deprived of so much of which others have in excess, a sense of heritage, community, belonging, family and nationhood as well as giving them the essential tools to rise to the opportunities that life will offer.

35

So how can we improve the usefulness and quality of education, without yet another upheaval?

First we must drastically reduce the role of central government. Education is about detail. Governments are bad at detail and indeed have no business there. Publicly funded educational responsibility must be fully devolved back to local authorities, so that they answer to their electorate for the quality of public provision in their community. In turn teachers must be given the freedom to use their creative and vocational talent (or have their lack of it laid bare) to empower the rising generation with the best education that modern technology can provide in a free and open democracy. The broad curriculum can be set centrally in terms of what knowledge and skill should accumulate to children at given points in their thirteen year journey of learning, but all the detail of the how and in what form should be left to the people in the business.

Government fixes the corridors through which planes can safely fly, but no longer does it try to run airlines. Air travel has improved vastly, has become a lot cheaper and is available to many more in consequence. It is interesting to reflect that as central government has become less and less involved in running industries and utilities following privatisation, it has not grown smaller, but bigger. Its meddling hands can be found in every nook and cranny of life, either directly or through an endless list of quangos. This has to be redressed. Especially in education.

This change to local governance would require little if any change in organisation as the structure is there and so are the people. The difference is that they lack actual authority to mange proactively and they are implementers of government policy, rather than initiators of policies devised locally to meet both aspiration and social need. This development would have little effect on the new group of Academies, Trust and Foundation schools as these are essentially a type of state funded independent school.

It would make a notable difference to all other state schools under LEA management, enormously shorten lines of communication, simplify decisions, reduce the demands on governors and, very important, cut the cost of the Whitehall ministry which could be significantly shrunk. Some authorities would be better than others at this role, but with the vigorous inspection regime now in place with very little adjustment, basic standards would be safeguarded. Poor performance would be punished at the ballot box.

The present structure of OFSTED is sound. The only adjustment necessary would be in the format of presentation. At the moment this follows the fixed format so beloved by modern governance and is required to reach judgements of performance which are either Satisfactory Good or Outstanding for each department. This is rather limiting, especially as more diversity develops in the school system and different schools aim for different objectives. I would favour switching to a points system out of ten in each area allowing for more subtle judgements, with an overall percentage for the final tally.

This is a convenient moment to look at examinations. As I write this (changes are in the offing and some have happened) the tally appears to be SATS at Key stages 1 and 2 with 3 already dropped. Then it is GCSEs followed one year later with AS levels and a year after that with A levels. There are also available new Diplomas as well as the International GCSE and the International Baccalaureate. Most state schools are working to GCSE and A Levels, the latter currently divided into AS and A2. This is not an exhaustive list as there other vocational and specialist variants. I am quite comfortable with the feeling that there are now far too many exams and too much emphasis on exam grades *per se* rather than knowledge in depth.

I would drop the remaining SATS. These are too prescriptive and provide very little motivation for pupils or teachers. Their main use is in school league tables, another obsession of modern central government. I would replace them with a formal Graduation, American style from Primary school, which would divide into Graduation, Graduation with Merit and Graduation with Distinction. This would all be based on the accumulation of work and its quality over the whole period of primary education, run by each school and supervised by the LEA, overseen by OFSTED. There would be no centralised exam, though there naturally would be tests along the way set by the school itself.

This would initiate pride in achievement for everyone and provide reward for effort at the end of this important foundation in the education journey. It would offer better motivation for children as well as parents and teachers. At a formal ceremony the young graduates would receive both a Graduation Certificate and a Medal, bronze, silver or gold (fake!) according to achievement. All pupils in the school as

231

well as all parents would assemble each year for the ceremony so that the younger pupils would be motivated through seeing the accolades to their seniors. This first achievement would be recorded online as part of the individual pupil's Educational Achievement Record if at some point the civil service learns how to install a functional computer programme without first wasting hundreds of millions.

Next and more controversially I would abolish GCSEs. I would replace this exam, the failure of which overall is measured by the fact that fewer than fifty per cent of students overall gain five passes A*- C including the essential maths and English. Instead there would be another Graduation, this time of Secondary Education, based upon work from age eleven to sixteen. This would cover all the core subjects and would allow the same three levels as at primary school. Everyone at whatever school, American style would graduate.

In addition, for the more academically gifted, there would be a choice, I suspect depending on school, of the International GCSE or the International Baccalaureate. These internationally recognised exams would carry students forward to university. For the vocational and practical students wanting more than Graduation the new Diploma programme could offer the basis a good way forward. AS and A levels would fade out as more schools offered the IGCSE and the IB.

Most exciting of all, by making each school responsible for its own graduation programme (within laid down parameters but with scope for choice) parents and pupils would be able to opt for the school offering the path best suited to their talents. This would give LEAs much better scope for meeting local need. Meanwhile the switch to the internationally recognised exams, already under way in the private sector, would give the academic stream a much more valued outcome. It would also severely restrict the ability of Whitehall to meddle. In the long term that would be the greatest benefit of all.

It has become clear that with the introduction of league tables and other measures to compare performance and with the current practice of funding all schools on a per pupil basis, some schools emerge much stronger than others and it is to these that ambitious parents naturally flock. There are now reports of surveillance cameras, espionage, false addresses and better off families instructing lawyers to manage applications to best advantage. This is not what public education is for or about and this will have to change. So too will the flawed assumption that any form of selection is bad.

I would favour a change in the rules. First residents within the catchment area of the school would have a right to attend, those longest resident with the first priority. Any surplus places would go to those from outside the area by selection interview by the school, with absolute power vested in the school and with no appeals procedure. The head of the school and their staff must have the right of decision of how to fill vacancies in the interests of their school, dependent on the interests of the school overall.

Second, as the system of graduation develops and as different schools specialise in vocational or academic courses I would have a benign selection programme to try and fit the pupil too the course. This would happen at the conclusion of primary education and would be reassessed at age fourteen to allow any change of direction. This would make the learning process an exciting and meaningful process for all children throughout their education. It would stop the grade chasing which has created the illusion of standards at the expense of learning.

36

Teaching is the core of education and, as so many surveys show, the quality of education relates directly to the ability of teachers. It does not depend on national curricular, processes, procedures or programmes, or inspections, or parents, or environment. All these things can play some part and if they are all favourable, weak teaching can be masked, achievement levelled to a satisfactory outcome which will get through OFSTED with controversy avoided.

This route will always produce the least challenging outcome, will fail the gifted and offer little to the disadvantaged. But good teachers, freed from direction of detail and free to innovate and inspire, can transform life prospects for the young in a way no other profession or organ of governance can ever hope to. The quality of every other category of human engagement in the future depends on the quality of teaching now. You cannot have students who make good doctors or lawyers or engineers unless their potential as been developed by good teaching. More fundamental is the stark fact that you will not make good teachers from those who have not been taught well themselves.

In transferring back to teachers the right to exercise their professional skill and judgement unhindered by central prescription, it follows that we must demand of them the required level of knowledge, aptitude and skill which must be the basis of their success in the classroom. No poorly performing teacher must be allowed to remain in post at the expense of the cohort of students struggling with the inadequacy of their performance in class. Every child has a finite number of days in which to learn and not one must be wasted giving a teacher priority over the taught.

As a governor I have watched teachers who either cannot teach or cannot control or both mess up the prospects of their students, especially those most disadvantaged, whilst management shuffled about mentoring and counselling and finally beginning the rigmarole of competency proceedings, whilst all the time these teachers carried on ruining the chances of their hapless classes. Everybody else gets fired if they cannot do their job and teachers are no different. Maybe they can be offered career assessment and retraining as a last resort, but they cannot be allowed to continue teaching in class.

So, teachers would get the freedom they deserve and from which all will benefit, but in return they must accept the responsibility that goes with it. They must have the qualifications, the knowledge and the aptitude for the job and be able to show they do it well. In return they must be better paid. Simplifying the whole system and removing huge swathes of Whitehall fiefdom will free up resources. These should be diverted to give teachers a pay structure which recognises their value to the whole of society.

37

Unfortunately far too much political capital and administrative effort has been used over the last decades of the issue of school type. Most, but not all, agree that the phasing out of the grammar schools was a mistake. The bigger mistake may actually have been the phasing out of the secondary moderns. These schools provided a really good basic education for children who were not academic or who were destined to life in trade rather than in the professions. Funnelling everybody through what has at times amounted to no more than a mediocre academic education whether they wanted it or not has short changed everybody.

There is no doubt that the either or selection at eleven was often unfair and caused bright children and late developers to miss out on the opportunities which flowed the way of the grammars if they failed to get into one. Although it was possible to move from secondary modern to grammar later, it was not an easy leap and many were never even offered the chance. The solution ought to have been to offer a middle road to enhance the secondary modern, rather to throw away the jewel in the crown. The nation paid a heavy price for this political blunder.

There are now quite a number of differing types of school in the state system and properly developed and adapted they should provide the flexibility to give children at every level and from every background the very best opportunity for a good start in life. If it can be assured that the less academically able get a really gold standard practical education, we should not shy off allowing a degree of selection to ensure the right children are in the best environment for their needs.

Recently a government sponsored inquiry, led by a former cabinet minister and containing a cross party group of luminaries among its members concluded that children from the less well off backgrounds stood less chance of making it into the professions. This element of a skilful investigation caught the headlines and it was around this that the media buzz was centred. There is something wrong here. As this narrative has already hinted and will further explore, we do not need more lawyers or top civil servants or whatever. We have far too many already. The excessive rise in the numbers of certain professions and their grip upon far too much of daily life and business has been detrimental to society as whole and will have to be reversed.

We do need doctors, but we need leaders, scientists, engineers, technicians, chemists, physicists, environmentalists, biologists and countless other gifted contributors to the fabric of society upon whose brains the survival of the human race and the quality of life will in future depend. To fill this ever growing requirement, whom you know must be a useless attribute. What you know must count. Knowledge, skill, commitment and the charisma to lead are blind to class and colour and deaf to social advantage.

We must nevertheless ensure that the provision of education out of taxation and free of cost at the point of delivery is of a standard to deny any advantage to those who chose not to use it. That must be the goal.

Blueprint

1 **Government should provide resources from taxation** and act as final trustee of the nation's educational standard.

2 **Government must not run education**, nor prescribe its format, nor interfere or engage in its management.

3   The running of state education should be returned to Local Government

4   The professional role of teachers must be restored.

5   There are currently far too many exams with too much focus on grades.

6   There should be a formal Graduation based upon the accumulation of work rather than set exam from both Primary and Secondary schools as the main and universal goal.

7   For the academically gifted the IGCSE or the International Baccalaureate should replace GCSEs and A levels

8   The syllabus of primary education must become broader based to provide a proper knowledge foundation.

9   Whilst Academy, Trust, Foundation and similar semi–independent schools should continue to be by pupil numbers, LEAs must be free to directly finance some schools according to community need.

2010
A Blueprint for Change
Part 6
Chapters 38-44

Quality of Life

I have led an unexceptional life in which my immediate family has been the main focus and in which there have been good and bad times, achievements and failures. There was, though, a period of eleven years when I was a full time house-husband looking after two young children, the youngest of whom had a rare congenital condition little understood by modern medicine. This gave the added challenge of twenty four hour care to nurture a life that hung by a thread.

Looking back on that hugely demanding experience I can say with all conviction that if I were put upon this earth for that and that alone, my life would have been fulfilled. I can also say that life for all of us in our little family with its brave but frail inspiration, had a quality quite unlike anything I had known before or known since that battle for life was lost. Afterwards all of us were left with something special. For me, I knew that I had touched the essence of life.

When I became re-connected to normal everyday life, I was shocked to discover how little its quality featured in general aspiration. This is why I have written this part. It is not about philosophy, but about the nuts and bolts of some of the ways in which we live.

38

The quality of life is now a widely used term, defining different things at different times in varying circumstances. In its general sense most people are comfortable with the phrase, though when it comes to the specifics, meaning is much harder to define. In this chapter I will try to explore what might be called the structure of our modern lifestyle, to try and determine whether any useful changes can be made to lift the value of life's experience for ordinary people. Much of human happiness comes from within and to explore that requires a book of philosophy or religion. This is not such a book. Nevertheless the way society is organised and the codes by which it governs itself can and do affect wellbeing in a very real sense.

There are many who hold that the quality of life today is not as good as at some point in the past, perhaps the nineteen sixties or even fifties. This must depend on the measure. Home comforts are now better, but transport, judged in time and simplicity from getting from one place to another, is worse. What has changed dramatically is the value we place on life itself. Nowadays the whole nation stops to grieve each time a serviceman is killed on active duty and when these deaths reach double figures there is a real sense of anxiety about the justification for the war responsible.

This is a new and in my view hugely admirable development. It was not always the case. In the Falklands war the exultation of victory was little dimmed by the two hundred and fifty five dead of the armed forces in seventy two days. In the Second World War over sixty two thousand civilians were killed and three hundred and twenty six thousand military. These figures appear almost beyond comprehension by today's standards, yet are dwarfed by the close on one million military and civilian dead for Britain alone in World War One. We have now made a great advance in civilised values.

No longer do we accept death, mostly of courageous young men, as a necessary instrument of policy and we recoil from the blood letting of previous centuries. We will tolerate loss of life just, but only just and we judge it no longer in hundreds, or thousands or tens of thousands, but individually one by one. Right across Europe, although substantial armed forces are maintained by most countries for defence of their borders, there is a reluctance to commit troops to risk on foreign fields; indeed it is politically impossible in many cases. This leaves the main burden to the U.S and ourselves.

This renewal of acceptance of the *value* of life has, curiously, been accompanied by a fading understanding of the meaning or *purpose* of life. In part this is due to the much wider exposure, through technology, of all people to the many different aspects of life in different cultures, when in earlier times simple truths and close communities were the majority experience. The rise and rise of the retail economy with its message that happiness is the product of shopping and that possession brings fulfilment, has a played a part in this shift.

There is a structural reason for the materialistic drift. It is less dominant in communities where faith in religion is still a part of everyday life. This does not mean that those who possess faith in the main possess nothing else. Most are just as acquisitive as everyone else, but they value possessions as part of experience, not part of life.

39

What we might call the spiritual health of the England is entrusted, constitutionally, to the Church of England. Many people feel that is has fallen down badly on the job. In the days when religion was the only truth and the driving force of politics, Elizabeth I put together the Church of England to reflect the beliefs of the moderate majority, some catholic, some protestant, in a format acceptable to both. Her structure survived the Civil War and the Glorious Revolution (more a coup than a revolution I think) and became a homely pillar of life, for some just baptisms, weddings, funerals and church at Christmas and Easter; for others a more devout acceptance of a fuller and deeper faith.

The interesting thing about the Church of England used to be the rather loose nature of its core beliefs. Obviously a Christian church, it nevertheless allowed a wide measure of freedom to its congregations to make their own interpretations of the traditional articles of faith and theology. This was the basis on which it was founded. Those who believed in the sacrament were free to go to Holy Communion at eight on Sunday mornings, those who did not could attend Matins at eleven, a service following the Book of Common Prayer, in use for centuries, and during which the sacrament made no appearance.

Some of these churchgoers believed in all the teachings, some in very few. This did not really matter, because although the overt purpose of the church was to prepare for the life hereafter, the main emphasis of its teaching fell upon the Christian code for life on earth in the here and now. Founded upon the Ten Commandments with later illumination from the Gospels these threads formed the yarn which held the fabric of society together. There was flexibility to adjust values as society became more enlightened, tolerant and scientifically informed. Eventually, of course, the numbers of the unbelievers grew to overshadow the believers, helped a good deal by the wanton slaughter of two world wars which caused people to question the motives of a supposedly caring God.

There was here some confusion of interpretation. The original teaching said what could be achieved by following a certain moral and ethical track. It did not say that rescue was guaranteed if whole societies left the rails, nor did it ever say that belief alone was sufficient to gain redemption. Now the so called Evangelicals have the upper hand, services have drifted from the Elizabethan tradition to a

249

more modern interpretation which puts much more emphasis on the importance of faith. Whilst this helps re-establish the core theology at the heart of fundamental Christianity, it narrows the usefulness of its values, because these become conditional upon belief.

It also turns the believers in upon their theology and its interpretation and away from their mission to set a standard for the conduct of life within society. They begin to argue among themselves. Media coverage of rows over gay bishops and women priests appear often to fly in the face of tolerance and don the full cloak of prejudice of the very worst kind; prejudice against people because of what they are.

This turns liberal minds (and spirits) well and truly off. It leaves the great example of basic humanity and common care shrouded in a dark and forbidding shadow, leaving the authority of the church diminished. These distasteful arguments about the nature of people are not the same as those which surround issues such as abortion or contraception or divorce. These latter are lifestyle issues which will always divide, which involve choice and for which the best outcome is to agree to differ with tolerance for the other view. There is no such leeway in outright prejudice against people for their genetic make up.

It is a fact that any religion or faith is free to adhere to whatever tenets it chooses and people can interpret scriptures in their own way and have faith in what they find. Christianity is divided into three great components, the Roman Catholic, originating from the Western Roman Empire, the Orthodox originating from the Eastern Roman or Byzantine Empire and the various Protestant churches and groupings, of which the Church of England was once the most liberal and inclusive. If it determines to follow a path which becomes prescriptive and censorious it will gather narrow though devoted appeal, but lose its ability to act as the broad spiritual lead of the nation. That is why and when it will find itself disestablished.

This would be a pity to some and a good thing to others. Either way the present Established status seems to many to be irrelevant or pointless. It is up to the Church of England to give it point. It may find its own future brightens. It may be that society as a whole would then have a firmer foundation on which to build new more inclusive values. If my ideas for the reform of the House of Lords found favour and the House of Faith became a reality, it may no longer be realistic for the Church of England to have Established status. It would certainly face challenge and competition. That would be good.

40

In the immediate post-war period and through the nineteen fifties, a major political catchphrase was the Standard of Living. The Labour and Conservative parties, who dominated parliament, traded polices to show that each was more to be trusted with continuing improvement than the other. Yet we hear little about this now. Some have achieved a living standard, judged in terms of possessions, status, lifestyle and career far exceeding expectations of those days.

Others have sunk to a level that was believed then to have been risen above permanently. Bright new estates built then, finally clearing slums left from Victorian times, have become new and much more deadly slums of a lawless subculture were a new underclass festers in envy, sustained by benefits, drugs and burglary, ignored by the rest of society and exploited by the barons of organised crime.

The conclusion is clear. It is not the standard of life which is the key but the quality. Improving the quality for the underprivileged ought to be the first aim of all political forces, since this imbalance between the have an awful lots and the have almost nothings cannot be sustained. Sooner or later there will be rupture. In the past this meant strikes or in bad times even riots. In future it will mean terrorism.

In the past the problem was the exploitation of the working classes. Now it is the exclusion from the glitter of the retail society of those who have no work, have never worked and on present form never will. Whilst the upwardly mobile live in a cone of fulfilment and satisfaction, these hapless souls at the bottom of the pile live in a vacuum from which all the best that modern life has to offer has been sucked. Into that chill void who knows what malevolent doctrine will seep, or how it may nurture perceived injustice to weld a force to threaten all which it coverts and has thus far been denied?

Throwing benefits at the problem will not help, though is in the short term necessary to keep lives together. Neither is it god enough to say that it is all their own fault and they should make the effort. In the majority of cases how they got there is of little importance. It is getting them out that counts. Nevertheless closing off the route to this deprivation is important strategically if the problem, which affects real people with real life experience at this grim margin, is to be overcome, so let us begin there.

It is the worst condemnation of our education system that it does so little at the start of these lives to steer them on a better path. We really do have to organise more useful education, following a more inspirational pattern, to equip all youngsters with the basic skills, both socially academically and vocationally to be able to play a full and useful part in the life of our country and thus gain focus and fulfilment of their own.

We have made such a mess of this over the last thirty years that a frightening minority come from entirely dysfunctional homes where knowledge and learning in the wider sense is unknown; where a moral code of whatever persuasion or faith is unheard of; where vision of the future is blurred by bad diet, smoking, alcohol and increasingly drugs and where, perhaps worst of all, a sense of belonging to the wider community is replaced by the reality of exclusion from it.

This dreadful situation must not put us off, but act as a spur to a more realistic and enlightened effort to redeem this shameful sore at the heart of twenty first century England. If not motivated by a Christian urge to alleviate suffering at least we need the wit to see that failure here will cause the sore to grow to a boil and then to a tumour which will threaten the very survival of all that we think is good about our lives today. This is not just a problem for politicians. Churches, Industry, communities, indeed all who have the power to act need to find the will to do so.

Even if we can assume (a big if) that the education prospects of these young people become transformed by a more enlightened approach, there must await them realistic prospects of employment, which will add value to their lives and to the whole community. Here quite a serious rethink is needed. At the end of the day, however many initiatives and programmes are devised, the plain fact is that a community needs a centre of employment with sufficient jobs for all who can work, a school with a curriculum designed for the needs of the young people of the area, a shop or shops, a pub, a post office and a surgery for medical support.

It needs a police officer in residence to deter crime and act as a rock of support to the law abiding majority. The knowledge of such an officer, living in the community, knowing the residents and watching the comings and goings would provide intelligence for C.I.D officers of exceptional quality. Add to that local church leaders and councillors and you have a rounded community which is self supporting and becomes and integrated asset to society as a whole.

Times have changed! No they have not. Times have not changed on their own. We have changed them with decades of muddled initiatives and confused thinking. The essence of community has not changed since the dawn of man. This signal truth should be at the heart of public policy. Communities must have within them contained all the elements of productive life or they founder and become public service dependencies, ghettos of a trapped underclass, festering in discontent, becoming progressively less able to contribute and a drain upon the wellbeing of that better life from which they are denied.

Efficiency drives, privatisations, closures and a vast export of straightforward manufacturing jobs overseas have combined to bring this imbalance. The fact that the economy has to have its financial structure operating in what might be called harmonious tension without excessive strain developing has already been discussed in an earlier chapter. In a modern developed society this principle must apply to social factors also. Standard of living and quality of life must be in balance. Organising an economy requires the recognition right at the outset that the purpose of the economy is a social outcome. A prosperous society is a better one. This cannot be sustained with unsound finance. But sound finance cannot be sustained with an unsound social structure beneath.

The underclass is the social result of the very policies and practices which eventually caused the banking collapse. The two are opposite faces of the same coin. The basic law governing all this is the rather simple reality that broadly an economy based on consumption must produce what it consumes. Our problem is that economic activity is governed by what people spend on goods, but now almost none of those goods are made by the economy buying them. Where there were once factories making almost everything needed to sustain daily life, there are now retail parks or empty spaces. Relatively full employment was maintained until the global financial crisis, but doing what? How many of these jobs contribute to real (rather than borrowed) wealth and how many of them drain it away?

The answers to these questions are beginning to emerge with the literally calamitous state of public finances both here and in the U.S. Both countries have borrowed too much and spent it on things made in China. China has relied too much on selling whatever it could make overseas and been willing to use the profits to lend the money to provide more purchasing power to its customers. Its savings dwarf those of everybody else. It will need to save less and spend more on its own infrastructure.

But here (and in the U.S) we have to reign in spending both private and public to reduce levels of debt which are essentially out of control. This will mean less activity in the High Street, higher taxes and huge cuts in government spending. This will further limit economic activity. The hardest hit will be those at the bottom of the pile.

The situation is made all the worse by the fact that far too many people employed have not been *usefully* employed. Their jobs either do not really exist or their existence is a drain on the system. We have lived increasingly in the last decades in the belief that it was clever and useful to make money. This is impossible. Money does not actually exist. It is a measure to denote value and can be exchanged for goods or services. It cannot be made any more than it is possible to make centimetres or inches or kilograms. All of these depend on there being something of substance to measure or weigh. We seem to have lost the economic plot.

We shall not find it until we begin to employ our greatest resource, our own working population, in producing a good deal of what we need. Our money will then come to measure real value and increase as our output and assets increase in volume. Provided we do not try to do this by simply using borrowed money to inflate existing assets, which is an illusion for the borrower and leads to cash flowing from west to east, we shall begin to rebuild the core of our national wealth. The standard of living will then start to rise, for some more than others, but the quality of life will improve for all.

Above all our leaders must recognise, and we must accept, that a prime goal of public policy is a motivated society whose quality of life is an essential outcome and where the most precious resource of all, human endeavour, is neither exploited nor wasted.

41

It is only necessary to watch one of the many superb nature programmes on television to discover that in almost every species there is a remarkably organised domestic order which ensures successful breading and nurturing of offspring. Such was once the case in our own society. More recently the fashion has been to engage child minders, nurseries and the like to free both parents to follow their careers.

This is not a new idea. The upper classes employed nannies and governesses to manage their children, sent the boys off to boarding school at a tender age, and organised within their substantial homes a completely separate household and domestic routine for their offspring. The motivation for this arm's length approach to family upbringing was not pressure of work but the opportunities of the social calendar. The more one drifted down the wealth and class structure, the closer parents came to the upbringing of their children, until somewhere round the middle of the middle classes, parents took full control.

Of course the model was marriage first and children next. Dad worked, mum looked after the children, ran the home and though not recognised (even in law) as the head of the family, she was, without doubt, the inspiration which held it together. Not only was her contribution to society grossly undervalued but added to this injustice was the insult of implied inferiority. If she did work her pay would be significantly less than a man doing the same job.

There has been a great crusade to bring the rights of women at all levels, but especially in educational and career opportunities, up to the same level as men of equal ability. More has to be done and male chauvinism still exists. Nevertheless young women expect to have careers and many rise to the top. It is all a far cry from the days, not long ago, when the woman's place was in the home. This is all good news, but as with all good news, there is a downside. If the woman's place is no longer in the home, is anyone keeping the home as the centre of the family or has the home become a house where people live together following separate lives which meet but never touch?

There are countless families were both parents work and where the children enjoy a caring as well as loving environment in which the family values itself collectively and each other individually. Parenting is of the best and the benefit to the children shows in both their achievement and behaviour. Sadly there are now a great many families which fall short of this ideal and a growing number which are entirely dysfunctional.

This is not a class issue, as although the poorest families are under the greatest pressure from which they cannot escape, some of the best off make choices which lead to their failure to provide a stable home for their offspring. Sadly nothing in human affairs is straightforward and reform of injustice invariably leads to new issues previously unforeseen. This is why those engaged in national leadership, not just politicians, need constantly to adjust advice, example and opportunity to keep society on a progressive course which is both balanced and sensitive.

Over the last few years there has been a tendency, when something is seen to be wrong, to demand action, causing the government to introduce new regulations or laws to deal with the problem. This has led to jibes about the nanny state. It is now a fact that there are far too many laws affecting everyday life, when not law, but habit needs to change. We often look at the particular without a clear view of the general.

It is now clear that the part played by women as homemakers and carers for their own children was grossly under valued. It followed that when the opportunity came for women to pursue full time careers, so little value was placed upon their domestic contribution hitherto, that no thought was given as to how their place was to be filled. That everything can be handed over to day care nurseries or that it is good for children to manage without parental care in the daytime in the pre school period, is at best a solution of necessity and at worst a complete disaster.

There is no doubt that it is right for women to have the same opportunity to work in any field of endeavour as men and be paid on the same universal scale. That is emphatic. It is equally emphatic that it is not good for children to be denied the benefit of parental care during most of their waking hours in the years before full time school begins and in the holidays after it does. It does not mean the mother must fill this role. The father can be just as effective as a carer. But when couples decide to have children they have an obligation to think all this through.

There are many single parents for whom this poses an impossible challenge and who need state help. But the state favours the parent working and the benefits are designed to drive him or her to that goal. This is completely incoherent. Looking after a young family, providing love, security, home cooking and parental comfort and guidance is the most valuable job of all. There is no greater calling. Done well it lays the foundation upon which the young citizen will build a worthy and worthwhile life as a net contributor to the advance of the whole of society. Money invested here to see this work done will save a lifetime of benefits and support.

Unfortunately the absurdly elevated cost of housing, coupled with the pressure on the population to maintain spending to sustain our retail economy, means that in the majority of families both partners have to work in order to pay the bills. This should not be. It is right that partners should have a choice if they both wish to work, provided they accept that they have an obligation to their children to provide good alternative care in their absence. It is not right that couples should be forced out of necessity to leave their children in other people's care just to achieve a basic standard of living.

All of this is a minefield full of danger for politicians. The number of campaigners and interest groups involved is significant. The range of conflicting interests is daunting.

265

Whatever course is advocated will bring a storm of protest from another quarter. Only a change of acceptance of what is best by the majority of society collectively will create the energy to bring about change. That may or may not happen.

If it does, it will need to be based upon the simple acceptance that there is no more important job in society than that of a good parent/carer. Organising the economy and its attendant aspirations to facilitate that undertaking so as to benefit the greatest possible number of children must be a central goal of public policy. Family life must be reset as the bedrock on which the pyramid of modern society rises and must be at the heart of our culture. This is the only sure way to ensure an improvement in the quality of life for all children and, in so doing, secure the quality of life for everyone.

42

As the borrowing binge turned to bust, as well as the obvious fear for the future, there was widespread unease among many that life had become unbalanced, values had become corrupted and the calamity befalling us all was the inevitable outcome of an earlier wrong turning. That wrong turning was shrouded in a rather misty consciousness, but it could have been connected to valuing what we had above what we are, admiring status above function, grade above effort, aggression above compassion, value over worth, spin over fact, all underpinned by the alchemist's delusion that money can be made rather than earned. Our economy had become dominated by the service and retail sectors driven by ever burgeoning financial services. This latter element collapsed upon itself in the greatest demonstration of mismanagement, exploitation and wishful thinking since the dawn of the industrial revolution.

Yet the question hangs in the air. Were the bankers greedy and ruthless exploiters of an innocent society's desire to better itself, or where these reviled financiers the product of a society which had lost its roots and was willing to pay any price and incur any debt in order to acquire more and more? To the pertinent question was it us or was it them,

them is the universal response. Yet were we truly innocent victims or were we fellow travellers to the great financial disaster?

There is no absolute answer to this. Clearly we were willing to go with the borrowing boom, or it would not have happened. That we were willing to do so is as much to do with the post socialism culture as it is to do with lack of judgement based on caution. The prevailing mantra since the end of the seventies has been that to own is to arrive and to spend is to invest. This could all be true if money to do these things is first earned. But to assert that buying assets at inflated values on borrowed money benefits anyone other than the lender is rubbish. Equally to go out and spend in the High Street or retail park is fine if you have the money, but to do it at the expense of savings or worse, to do it on credit, means that a burden must now be carried into a future for which little provision has been made.

All of this creates an atmosphere of pressure to provide the latest kitchen, car, holiday abroad, computer game, iphone and so forth, requiring parents to work all hours to meet the ever increasing commitments, so that children are left to bring themselves up, as their needs are judged in terms of what they are given, not how they are looked after. In the end there comes social and financial implosion, most of which is yet to happen.

This was not the aim of the new capitalism which took over from the tattered socialist economic model. Sadly in politics the outcome in the end rarely squares with the aim at the beginning. Although the standard of living has risen for the majority, the quality of life in the sense of the fundamentals; family cohesion, contentment, security, employment and future prospects, is often short of the experience of half a century ago. This cannot be a good thing.

Whether change happens is in part the responsibility of political leadership, but only part. To achieve a seismic shift in the values to which society as a whole gives priority requires an equal shift in public mood to drive the politics forward. This was the case for the setting up of the welfare state and the extensive nationalisation programme of the immediate post war period. It was also true of the unravelling of this old style socialism during the nineteen eighties. If we as a nation now want to see our quality of life judged by human values rather than economic data, we will have to indicate that to follow such a path of reform is the new agenda informing our voting intentions.

43

A rather odd development, which greatly affects the quality of everyday life, certainly in the ease with which it can be lived, is the rise and rise of due process. One might have supposed that as the frontier of the socialist way of doing things was rolled back there would be fewer and fewer controls and directives on everyday life, not more and more. It is no longer possible to organise a financial transaction without proving your identity, your address and your regular use of public utilities. When challenged, a building society clerk will explain that it is to do with 'money laundering'.

Other transactions are made extraordinarily complex because of 'the data protection act'. Human Rights, noble in aspiration and vital in the protection liberty and free speech, somehow prevent discipline in the classroom, while school playgrounds, where in the past healthy knock about taught both tolerance and toughness, are now regarded as places of hazard. Employers find it difficult to select from divers applicants without committing some act of discrimination and in any case face an unimaginable number of regulations both national and European in the daily conduct of their business. An ever growing number of regulators, the initials of their various titles combined to make silly words like *Ofwat,* fill the media with news of their latest investigations into the pricing structure of whatever it is they supervise, yet the price, quality and reliability of these utilities seems never to have been less satisfactory.

The list of laws and regulations is endless. Most people have not a clue what they all are. The number of regulatory bodies and other quangos regulating and monitoring our daily lives is unknown but enormous. The number employed in these activities rival those in the armed services. The purpose of it all is to protect our interests, save us from risk, keep us safe, control everything we do and ensure that our lives run smoothly and do not fall into the unexpected.

The price we pay, quite apart from the drain on the public purse, is the highest rate of crime, the worst functioning government, the greatest infringement of personal liberty and the lowest quality of daily life in living memory. No longer is anyone allowed to make a judgement, reach a decision or commit to a course of action without a ludicrous adherence to some due process designed to ensure success, which in practice achieves the opposite. Wisdom is

271

off the approved list and has been replaced by celebrity. An ominous word has crept into public jargon, *compliance*.

If we are upstanding citizens with no blemish on our record, our names on the voting roll, our council tax paid, our national insurance number valid and our behaviour law abiding, why should we have to prove to a whole raft of businesses and other agencies who we are? Is it not their function, if suspicious of our bona fides, to prove who we are not?

Sadly they have no choice. It is not their fault. The fault lies in the nature of the legislation which has been piled onto the statute books over the last thirty odd years and especially in the last decade. It also has a root in the way the laws are administered. In the less recent past the political agenda was driven by two overriding priorities. Winning world wars, or in the case of the cold war stopping one breaking out, and advancing social justice to smooth the suffering and inequality stemming from the industrial revolution and building of an Empire. These were all absorbing big ticket issues, keeping government busy.

Largely these tasks were completed, at huge human cost from two wars and in much human misery through an often slow pace of social reform. Thereafter government turned its surplus energy towards the more ordinary elements of everyday life, looking not at fundamentals but at standards. So having ensured that everyone had an opportunity to receive free education for example, government became concerned with the quality of that education. Although the intention is laudable, the practice is flawed.

This is because government is a much more limited institution than it likes to admit. It consists, even in its current overblown state of little more than a hundred people supported by the civil service, controlling the lives of sixty million. It has two options. The first is to organise the police and armed services to oppress the population and keep them in line. We have spent centuries spilling our blood to advance the leading edge of the freedom, so that is not a way forward for any British government for which its own overthrow is not the aim.

The second is to enact an ever increasing number of laws and regulations which place the onus upon the regulated to enforce them. This is the route which government has chosen to follow and which we have, thus far, allowed it to travel.

273

I will give two examples. Health and Safety regulations require schools (and every business or public organisation) to place safety above everything. Risk must be reduced or eliminated requiring the curtailment or modification of a huge range of activities previously regarded as run of the mill. Failure to comply, note the word *comply*, renders the school not only liable to criminal prosecution, but also to be sued for substantial damages in a civil court.

Likewise all the identification issues, of which I have already complained, when opening a savings account arise because of the bank or building society being made liable to prosecution if it handles money for laundering. In both these cases the organisation is being required to both administer and for practical purposes, police the law.

It follows that both education authorities and financial institutions spend a lot of money fulfilling these responsibilities and in so doing curtail activities in the playground and inconvenience legitimate customers. Yet to what purpose?

Accidents still occur and vast sums of money are laundered. Why do we have these laws? Is it not reasonable to suppose that any school would wish to make sure that its pupils were not exposed to needless harm? Is not learning about risk and being able to judge it part of education? Surely this is a matter for the schools themselves? No business, fun fare, railway or whatever will survive for long surely if they keep harming their customers. Surely it is a matter of fact that we want to protect those on whom we depend in a civilised society. Is it really a matter of law? Ought the government to be here at all?

Likewise would it not be just as efficient, perhaps even more so, to ask financial institutions to notify the authorities if they suspect money laundering rather than making them criminally liable in the process? The law already provides for the notification of a suspected crime anyway. It would certainly be more customer friendly.

It is possible to sight one example after another in this whole area of government not of our country but of our lives. Strike up a conversation in a pub, a supermarket checkout queue or at a bus stop to discover just how deep public anger seethes at the way our lives have been diminished and our worth devalued by this overreaching style of government, for which all political parties must shoulder blame.

Not only is the English person's word no longer their bond (to update the old saying to a modern politically correct version), but trust generally is undermined. The notion that if the *process* has been followed all is well with the end, leads people to become cynical and distrust everyone, their leaders especially.

The older citizens think nostalgically of easier days and wonder where things are headed. The young exploit the system if they can, or if they cannot, exclude themselves from it. This is where the real danger lies. A deep unease rises in the depth of our consciousness, that our treasured word to express our condition, freedom, now has a hollower ring than it did before.

This is not a plea for government to be abandoned except at the loftiest heights, nor that society should be without laws governing its conduct, nor that public activities be allowed to operate at any standard no matter how ineffective or dangerous. It is a series of questions posed about the quality of the way we live and a plea for the return of common sense, judgement and wisdom as the qualities which inform both the nature of public policy and how society views the outcome. Above all we need to see a return of responsibility from government back to individuals and their communities.

44

Having looked critically in this chapter at the Church of England, an area usually off limits for an outsider, I now intend a look at the police, because they are our custodians of much that we value when assessing our quality of life. Let me begin by saying that I admire the police force hugely and I have no criticism of it. When it is criticised I think it is often unfair to do so, as the police are generally the victims of circumstance, like the citizens they seek to protect.

On a recent visit to the United States, I was struck by the wide range of separately organised (and armed) law enforcement agencies including the big city police forces familiar to devotees of T.V drama, to the County Sheriffs and Park Rangers, not to mention the traffic cops and state troopers. At first I felt this was a confusing muddle, but as I began to sense the relaxed atmosphere of the various communities I visited in out of town America, I was not so sure. When I discovered that two sets of friends, one from California and one from New England, never locked their doors at night or when they went out, I was astonished. Of course this is not the case everywhere, but in my own country I do not think it is the case anywhere.

I returned with a feeling that we have not, in this country, organised our police service in a way which is enough related to the huge diversity of modern policing needs and this is why, at a local level there is widespread dismissal of the quality of police protection in the community. Anyone who has had a minor break in either to their home or car will relate a lack of police interest and a complete failure to investigate the crime. Of course a record will be made and a crime number issued for insurance purposes and there will be, even in the minor cases, an offer of trauma counselling and victim support.

The relationship between the insurance industry and the police in minor crimes is one of curious, though unconscious dependence. The insurers can use crime statistics to ensure that every householder buys their product and the police, having authenticated the crime by giving it a number, can thereafter ignore it because the victim is receiving compensation for his loss. The alarm industry has burgeoned over recent years and works in concert with insurers who require an active system before insuring larger amounts. Unhappily in the more deprived areas were break-ins are common, householders cannot afford insurance so they go uncompensated. They may even know who the burglar is but feel too vulnerable to intimidation to say.

In the larger scheme of things these crimes are quite trivial, but they, or fear of them, certainly impacts the quality of the lives of the affected citizens. At the other end of the scale there is evidence of difficulty to get to grips with organised crime. Latest figure show that the organised crime industry, for that is what it has become, amounts to over £30 billion annually in the UK alone and employs several thousand people. Our newly formed British equivalent to the FBI, SOCA (Serious Organised Crime Agency) is focussed on countering this black economy, but it is early days. It is certainly the right move if it is properly resourced and targets its effort with accuracy.

In some facets of crime there is an increase in fear without there being a corresponding increase in actual offences. This is perhaps the key. The way we have organised our police services makes them too disconnected to local communities. We begin to see the problem if we look at how they are set up and what they do. They appear to be very good when acting as an emergency service, whether it is a local road accident or a major disaster. High profile crimes, such as murder or abduction, particularly of children, bring enormous public admiration for the dedication and thoroughness of the police effort. Their role in countering the terrorist threat and their success in making arrests has been significant.

Where I think the problem lies, is that we expect too much from one force. Of course, we have lots of police forces, one for every county or major city as well as the Metropolitan Police, but essentially they are all the same in one major respect; they all look after everything in their patch. I begin to feel that in this modern more sophisticated digital and electronic world we need several different specialist forces, rather than one which does almost everything. There are some specialist forces such as the British Transport Police, Customs Officers and the new U.K. Border Agency, but in the main the public is aware of one force.

Whilst leaving our current police forces as the heavy duty crime fighting arm of the state, I would remove responsibility for two activities. The first and obvious improvement would be a national traffic police responsible for everything to do with road traffic. This is a very demanding part of the police function, though generally the relationship with the public is quite different than that which exists or should exist with local policing. It takes significant manpower resources, which can be quickly mobilised to attend any motoring emergency, but while this is happening in a blare of sirens, the neighbourhood is often left without visible cover. Even if there is no connection the community is reminded of its lack of local law enforcement, by the evident commotion in the distance.

The second change I would propose is the setting up of a Community Police Service as a quite separate and separately managed police force. Its officers would patrol on foot, live in the community they patrolled and protect it from criminal activity at all levels. It would be subject to local democratic control through existing local authority structures. Although fully authorised police officers, the function of these men and women would be to prevent crime rather than to solve it. Their observations would provide invaluable intelligence for crime busting operations of the more heavy duty police force and their local sensitivities would be invaluable in areas like child protection and domestic violence. To mark them out and restore confidence in every neighbourhood, I would have them uniformed in green rather than blue.

When I look back to my youth in a village in Kent, we had a police house, specially built, in the centre of the village

283

with a resident constable who was part of the community and who patrolled the village and every country lane in the parish on his bike every single day. He knew everyone and everyone knew him. In the local town there was a police station open twenty four hours, manned by a station sergeant and several constables who patrolled everywhere night and day seven days a week throughout the year. People walked without fear on the streets and were safe in their homes.

Whatever rationale is advanced for the modern mobile and much more dramatic approach, there is no getting away from the fact that to achieve this by abandoning the old foundation of community policing had a hugely detrimental impact on the lives of ordinary law abiding people, especially the vulnerable and the elderly. It is time to restore the protection citizens have a right to enjoy. In the end the fight against crime will not progress until all communities and neighbourhoods become no go areas for criminals.

These are just a few of the issues that seem to me to be ripe for reform and which could have a positive impact on the quality of everyday life. Every reader will be able to think of countless others. Always when reform is proposed, the question of cost is a ready dampener to the hand of those who do not want to bother. But cost is real and has to be met from somewhere.

Overall government has become hugely too big, doing vastly too much at frightening cost and often with little positive impact. As a nation we have become prone to the cry that the government must do something every time an issue of public concern arises. It is largely our fault that government has become an industry and we look to it for the satisfaction of every need. This process must now reverse. Money, our money, needs to go where it matters.

Blueprint

1 **Government is too involved** in the detail of daily life

2 **People need to be allowed to exercise judgement,** rather than be required to follow process

3 **Spiritual needs must be given** equal weight to material values

4 **The quality of legislation must improve,** with its purpose more clearly defined and its benefits more stringently tested.

5 **The Police need to be reorganised to provide a visible and effective guarantee** of safety in the community, previously part of the British way of life.

6 **Personal freedom has been curtailed** by complex laws and unnecessary regulations and by perceived priorities of public security. This trend must be reversed.

7 **Self sufficient communities with employment,** education, health, law enforcement and recreational opportunities must be re-established as the bedrock of the social structure of the nation.

2010
A Blueprint for Change
Part 7
Chapters 45-54

A More Practical State

In the first six parts of this narrative I have explored some of the key issues which face our country and identified changes which I believe would deliver a better outcome. In this final part I want to explore the broad picture which would emerge if practical, rather than ideological, solutions were found. We shall revisit some issues already reviewed and come upon new ones.

The challenges rising before us, like an unexpected mountain range above the dawn mist, make our journey forward so much more hazardous than we expected so short a time ago. People feel let down by leaders who failed them, politicians who deceived them and bankers who exploited them. There is anger and frustration, stronger than at any time since World War Two. What we need now is not another ideology, nor adherence to some rigid dogma. The time for all that is past.

To move on, a practical approach is needed. Above all we need to understand that government is about big things. We need to be allowed manage smaller things ourselves.

45

Every so often as history unfolds a time arrives when the public mood ripens to a desire for major change. This has happened twice since world war two. In 1945 an exhausted but triumphant country gave Labour a landslide mandate to introduce democratic socialism, public ownership of utilities and transport and to introduce the welfare state. When they had enough of change the electorate put the Conservatives back, but only to adjust at the margin, not to alter the big picture. There was an ideological debate over whether free enterprise or state control could best deliver, but what was required was not in doubt. The political consensus sat left of centre. Thereafter the two main parties came and went alternately. Up to 1979, Labour and the Tories enjoyed separate periods of government totalling seventeen years each.

Then came another sea change. The old consensus fell apart. Left of centre had not delivered the same conclusive economic growth enjoyed by other countries in the West. The rising generation felt there must be better way. In came the Tories, this time led not by an emollient one nation patrician, but by the fiery radical Margaret Thatcher. At huge cost in unemployment, the destruction of the industrial infrastructure with the collapse of inner city communities and a certain dismissal of society of which there was said to be 'no such thing', the political agenda moved sharply to the right.

The left countered by moving further left and walked into electoral massacre, three times in a row. The fourth attempt when victory was widely predicted and over confidently expected turned to another bitter disappointment. If there were to be any chance of power again Labour would have to accept the unravelling of socialism.

Just as post war Conservatives had accepted its ascendancy in the fifties, so Labour abandoned a good deal of its baggage at the wayside and moved to the centre, now far to the right of where it had been before. This, at last, brought electoral triumph on a scale and longevity unknown before. For a time all looked well, but then disaster struck; the worst financial crisis in modern times followed by a deep and sudden recession. That was bad enough, when revelations about MP's expenses burst upon us. They had kept us in the dark while milking a lax and permissive system about which we knew nothing. This was the last straw. Not only had the financial system fractured, but Parliament was both incompetent and untrustworthy.

290

There is now a deep desire for renewal exceeding even that of 1945 in many quarters, but unlike then, or 1979, there is no alternative in waiting. There is no revolutionary moving from fringe to mainstream, no radical doctrine gaining ground. There are just the Tories, having moved back to the centre to gain electoral shine, offering a cautious but reasoned analysis of a less spendthrift approach, burnished with buzz words like openness and transparency. Nice people, a blend of new and old money, but do they have the answers?

There are other parties with the Liberal Democrats at the head, perhaps poised to enter a coalition in a hung parliament, but unlikely to break through to lead the government. They all talk of reform, but what do they mean? Do any of them really know what to do? Is this not one of those times when we need a real change with a new agenda, different objectives, new values, a seismic shift of what kind of society we want. Society does exist, very much so. It can be a good society or a bad society or to quote Lyndon Johnson, a Great Society. We, all of us, deep down know this. Society exists because society is us.

This time will have to be different. This time we will not be able to turn to a leader who comes with a plan to inspire, or to a creed which offers a better way and in which we can put our faith. We have to work this ourselves, by reminding our leaders that we are a sovereign people and our calls must be heard. This time the power is with us. Let us use it well.

46

The first thing to get right is the way we are governed. Too much of the current system is in disrepair. Too little of it is respected by the governed. It is not just expenses. It is the notion that parliament is some kind of club which confers rights and privileges upon its members and takes little notice of the electorate between elections. At elections the voters are bombarded with so much propaganda on which millions are frittered, but they are never told the truth. Everything in government is confidential, which is fine if it is personal or affects national security for real, but all wrong if it means the people are not being told what is really going on. Secretive government is incompatible with democracy, as we have already discussed.

Originally the crown ran the government and parliament restrained it and held it to account. This is how the American Constitution is modelled, with the President kept in check by Congress. We tell the people that we have a different but equally good democracy, but apart from electing the Members of Parliament, we barely have a democracy at all. This is because in parliament all the power of the crown has been taken by the government which then controls parliament through the whips. Locally in England except where there are elected Mayors, too much power has been transferred back to Whitehall, which is in turn controlled by the government. Only if it is in power with a very slim majority or falling apart generally does the government have to really take notice of parliament.

I looked at this in an earlier section. My proposals would produce a more modern, democratic and responsive structure. The age of the professional politician, in cosy with the establishment, spinning round the Westminster village at the behest of party bosses would be over. It has not served us well. We would have members of parliament truly representing the constituency in which they would live in their *only* home and coming to parliamentary sittings expressly to scrutinise and check the government.

These new parliamentarians would be men and women who had gained the respect of their communities and who in the true spirit of public service would be willing to give some years of their lives for a salary similar to a teacher. Many would belong to a political party, though maybe not all. They would not be willing to have themselves churned through the lobbies as fodder for a voracious government gorging itself on ever more legislation to give it ever wider power. Above all they would know that the purpose of government is not to run the country but to enable the country to run.

The object of democratic government is to create the conditions in which the country can run itself. When we say country we mean the people, for without them there is no country. When we say people we mean the ordinary people, not the political elite, whose day, much wasted, is over.

The government itself would have to be drastically slimmed down to a maximum of fifty ministers, of which a maximum of twelve would form the cabinet. The number of Departments or Ministries, currently twenty two would be cut by half leaving Home Affairs, Foreign Affairs, Treasury, Justice, Environment, Transport, Education, Agriculture, Health, Welfare and Defence. All the various necessary government functions would be grouped within those departments but the total remit of central government would be slashed. Much does not need government of any sort. For example Enterprise, Innovation, Families, and so on are not issues in which government can usefully become involved directly, although the effectiveness and competence of government overall will impact all these facets of life.

The function of central government is to collect and distribute financial resources to ensure the maintenance of the infrastructure and the provision of services in a fair and equitable proportion and to uphold the law and protect the peace. Local government should have the responsibility for the management of public services including education and health. No government at any level has the right to micro manage daily life and all government has the responsibility to ensure that none grow rich at the expense of or by exploiting the poor. Wealth creation is not only good but essential in advancing the standards of all the people, but it must be wealth creation and not sucking resources from the poor to the rich.

It is alarming to find that the gap between rich and poor has grown over the last decade, and dangerous when we discover that this has been achieved by plunging both the population and the country into debt at almost unmanageable levels. Little new wealth has really been created. There is more money in the system but it is worth less. Assets have been inflated in apparent value, but they are still the same assets. The process of reducing the value of money has been going on throughout modern times and kept at a very modest level no harm comes. But harm does come if the price of a basic commodity such as housing rises to the point where people have to borrow excessively to get a roof over their head. It is the bankers who profit and the ordinary wage earner who pays. Once again it is worth coming back to the theme that money is a measure. It is not true wealth. It is the only measure without a constant value.

Let me illustrate this is a simple way. Let us suppose we want to increase the value of our home. We could build on an extension to make the living room thirty feet long instead of its current twenty feet and this new feature would make the property more attractive and more valuable. What we cannot do is reduce the size of inches so that the old living room becomes thirty five feet long by reducing the size of the measure. Yet this is what we have been doing with money.

National government has a responsibility to create a social model which delivers a fair and efficient economic and social environment, which is caring not only for the weak among us but also for the increasingly fragile eco structure and allows the people to develop their lives to their highest calling in freedom. Some parts of this are best undertaken by the state, other parts by local communities and other parts by the people individually or collectively under the banner of free enterprise. It is the balance between these various potentially opposing forces which forms the traditional basis of ideological debate.

This is because government can operate many ideologies. On the left is socialism. On the right is capitalism. The former holds that the state should own and distribute; the latter that is the free market is best. As the current recession was brought on by an implosion of markets, the market economy has lost a good deal of its shine. Oddly there is no rush to socialism, maybe memories of its weaknesses are still vivid enough to deter.

Our politics have generally settled on a consensus sitting in the centre. All but the fringe parties are gathered here. Commentators talk about clear blue water opening up between them, but these waters are rivers not oceans. The argument is about the detail; to regulate more or less, to regulate by this authority or that one, to judge targets differently, to keep league tables but using different measures and so forth. There is debate on whether to spend more or less but on what there is general agreement.

Among the party leaders there are some personality differences and different social roots, but there is nowhere the contrast between Thatcher and Foot. Extremists argue that the centre is always the soft place where complacency rules, but never in history have extremists delivered lasting benefit. Nevertheless voters do not see the dramatic call to reform their anger seeks. They see instead a political class inward looking and shifty, tired and tatty putting self interest first, short of big ideas and drunk on little ones. There is a feeling that politics, like so much else, has become a process which is a law unto itself, immutable to influence by ordinary people.

47

We know that government cannot run our daily lives. We also know that government has now been so centralised and has so many regulators and other quangos as well as initiatives by the sack full that the whole enterprise consumes more than it delivers. We all have to work longer and spend more to raise the tax to pay for it without getting sufficient in return. This is because government is trying to do the wrong things.

If we look at the history of the last thirty years the picture is rather confusing. Until the recent crisis the economy had improved beyond recognition. Now, in terms of personal and government debt, things are worse than ever. The end of all those nationalised industries was very popular at the time and seemed the best way forward. The railways were the first to falter and are now part nationalised through Network Rail, the setting up of which had wide public support, following multiple failures at the privately owned Railtrack.

Suddenly the banking system began to totter, making the collapse of our financial system a real possibility, bringing ruin to every home in the land and the government had to rush to nationalise the worst and provide all manner of structural supports to hold up even the best. Millions are now paying for this corporate greed and commercial folly with their jobs and businesses, angry that the guilty made off with their spoils.

We look at our energy bills, spend our precious time ringing call centres to get a better deal, if we live in the country we keep candles handy for power cuts and if we get a decent summer face hosepipe bans because of water shortage in the very part of the country where the government wants more homes to be built.

Our privatised water company in the south was bought by the Scots then sold to the Spanish. Are we comfortable with this? Even more exotic is the takeover of British Energy, owner of most of our nuclear generating capacity and the largest generator of our electricity, to EDF which is owned by the French Government, so not only is it no longer private, it is back in state ownership, but not our own. Was all this supposed to happen?

Many, if not most, people are now uncomfortable with the private ownership of public utilities, because these essential elements of modern civilisation are in reality part of the infrastructure of the state, like the roads and the sewers and need to be available at cost, which must include future investment, as a key contributor to the essentials both of daily life and economic growth. At first, when they were privatised and ordinary people, many of whom had never bought shares, were able to profit from buying what seemed secure long term investments, things looked rosy.

As the City plunged its hands into the trough there began a series of takeovers and mergers which ended miles from the original idea. Then came the separation of production from supply and then the muddle of everybody selling everybody else's product, like gas from the electricity company and so forth, and additional providers buying bulk time and selling it on in the telephone service creating an illusion of competition when all it does is to increase cost and make quick fortunes out of nothing.

This is because the plain fact is that the electricity or water or whatever costs a basic amount to generate or pump and put into the system and that is the price consumers should pay. Now they pay for multiple company structures, takeovers and mergers, massive City commissions and lawyers' fees and of course regulators and quangos to stop the whole thing getting out of control. Moreover the claim that all this would lead to the required investment has not delivered. We are predicted to fall dangerously short of required generating capacity and attempts to bridge this with an energetic nuclear programme has brought forth cries from the industry for government subsidy. Bingo! Back to square one.

There is no doubt there were serious flaws in the way successive post war governments ran the nationalised industries and utilities. This was because the early model of public ownership in the socialist tradition required that the whole enterprise was owned directly by the state without shares and these enterprises were often starved of investment because of government cuts. Bureaucratic management methods led to inefficiency and sometimes poor service, especially in the case of the railways and the telephones, but not in the case of the nuclear generating industry which was the world leader.

Lessons have been learned all round. The practical way forward could be for the nation to own the majority block of shares in a single company providing the utility, but for the company to be managed like any other company with shareholders. Government would set policy but not manage. As long as the government held the majority of the shares there is no reason why other shares could not be purchased by individuals, pension funds and authorities seeking a safe haven for funds, which would have predicted value and not be part of the financial market. Like Network Rail these utilities would have to generate enough revenue to invest and renew and pay their costs but no more than that.

Such a practical approach would be very much in tune with the public mood which is a lot less comfortable with the so called market economy since it so spectacularly collapsed. It would create a sounder foundation for essential infrastructure, but to implement it now would be beyond the public purse. Demanding shares in exchange for subsidy would begin the process.

48

Although banks are not normally regarded as utilities, recent experience indicates that if not literally so, they are in many ways. Indeed when they were about to collapse the government had to step in with our money, no matter how much, to hold them up. That it was right to do this with Northern Rock which is more a building society than a bank, the Bradford and Bingley and one or two others is not disputed. There is a question, however, over the big two, the Royal Bank of Scotland and Halifax Bank of Scotland. There is also the question of providing bad debt insurance to the banking sector generally to stabilise the rickety system after wanton indulgence in financial recklessness.

Clearly the government was right to step in to save the depositors. I am among those who believe that this would have been better achieved by nationalising the retail banking sector right through and letting the so called investment arms of these banks, which in many cases are more like casinos, go to the wall. Paper fortunes would have evaporated and a good deal of non existent electronic money would have vanished. Shareholders would have taken a hit, but all the deposits would have been safe. That way the taxpayer would have ended up with the profitable arm of banking and the other part, relying on hysteria and financial innovation sometimes amounting to alchemy, would have been wiped out. There would have been a great shout of anguish and a bonfire of paper dreams, but it would have stopped there, because the crisis was the fact that there was nothing there in the first place.

What has happened is that the taxpayer is saddled with the losses, while the perpetrators of this monstrous attack upon the lives and livelihoods of ordinary people keep the profits. Not only is this entirely unjust, but it establishes a principle which will germinate the seeds of future disaster. This is because not only did these people feed themselves vast bonuses based upon illusory profits which were not actually there, but they now know that because they are too big to fail, when the next self inflicted crisis breaks they will have to be rescued again.

It is critical that we do not reward failure in this way, as this is what has happened, however it is dressed up. Risk takers must learn that they, not the taxpayer, will alone bear the burden of folly in future. That will do more than any regulator to curb excess. But we are left with a problem which will not go away.

It is this. The present plan is that at some point in the future the government will sell the shares in the rescued banks and make a profit for the taxpayer or at least get our money back. But after all the suffering of this recession and after saddling future generations with unprecedented public debt, we are left with the same basic insecurity at the heart of our economy. The banks are too big to fail and if they run into problems they bring us all down.

This then means that the taxpayer has to be the guarantor of the security of the system. The only way to do this properly and without sudden unsustainable cash calls is to own the retail banks in the first place. We should retain control of RBS and extend to majority control of HBOS, which foolishly includes Lloyds. As in present circumstances the cash is not there for a fair takeover of the others we should require both Barclays and HSBC to separate their retail arms from their investment arms and make it clear that the price of future rescue will be nationalisation, with serious losses for shareholders.

This is the only reliable route to a more secure future and is so important that it should be a priority of any incoming government. At present all the parties favour improving either the regulators or the regulations or both. Regulation is needed for an unsafe or unstable system, the more the risk the more the regulation. Better and much safer to have a secure system in the first place.

It was right to nationalise the Bank of England in 1946 and it is right to add retail banking to public control now. This is not a return to socialist theory. It is in response to practical necessity to guarantee the future security of our economy. The investment, or better called speculative, half of banking can carry on with its exotic activities at the financial cutting edge, some might call it a precipice, and from time to time one or other will go over the top and into the abyss. So be it. That is the right balance of risk and reward.

It is important to remember that before the great programme of deregulation and reform, known as Big Bang at the time, came into effect in 1986, the City of London contained various professional groupings which many criticised as class based and elitist, which in turn reduced the competitive edge, so that New York, Frankfurt and Tokyo began to challenge and suppress the City's world status in financial markets. These reforms were so successful that London not only regained its world class, but became the world leader. In concert with New York, whose businesses and systems are so closely linked to the City that they are at times hard to unravel, these two centres not only dominated the world, but did so with a financial model which was at the outset unstable and become ever more so until it exploded.

As we know the flash was blinding and the fallout global. Here, scorched and traumatised politicians talked of a global crisis as if it had happened elsewhere and we were just bystanders. In Europe people muttered darkly about the weaknesses of the Anglo/Saxon model and came close to the truth. The twin epicentres were London and New York. Down at the core was the flight from regulation, the so called Big Bang. It was right to de-regulate, open up markets and set entrepreneurs free. It was wrong to do this without first protecting the essential public utility of the normal banking system. This must now be secured.

49

This leads into the question of regulation overall. Regulation has become a self fulfilling industry over recent years. There are so many regulations governing modern daily life and business and so many regulators that they are reminiscent of the vast burial industry of ancient Egypt. This took up huge resources for a cause then believed critical to the life hereafter but now thought to be pointless. It has provided archaeologists with a wonderful insight into life and customs of the time. One wonders whether archaeologists and historians will in a few thousand years pick over fusty records dug up somewhere and marvel at the scale of regulation of the detail of life today. They may, too, conclude that it was all pointless and consumed huge resources to implement.

If there is indeed human life still remaining at such a time it will have learned that if the arrangements are right in the first place regulation is unnecessary, save for exceptional situations. We could profit from learning that lesson now. As government has distanced itself from the structural questions which shape society and concentrated ever more closely upon the rules by which life can be led, the volume of regulation has increased beyond imagination. Not only are there regulations but a vast array of quangos to police them. Big items have their own quangos like the utility regulators. Less specific issues, which in detail are all embracing, like Health and Safety, have the one, which penetrates everywhere.

This does several things to our society, economy and way of life. First and I think worst, it devalues personal responsibility and in many cases outlaws it. Second it inhibits judgement based on common sense and replaces it with the inflexibility of judgement by rote. These are the human effects. To give a simple illustration, people are no longer conditioned to look both ways before crossing the road; they wait for a green light. If the light is not there they lack the ability to judge the speed and distance of oncoming cars.

This has economic consequences because the people who make up society need much more support and are less well able to make their own way. This is a drain on resources and reduces the net worth of the contribution they do make. Another simple illustration; if it costs xy to get them to work but when there they contribute only y, things are not working out. The loss of personal initiative, willingness to accept risk and the ability to make judgements and be judged on their outcome, not only hobbles the individual and restricts freedom, but it hobbles the whole society and economy, which then moves forward with the wheezing uncertainty of an exotic but underpowered car.

This creates a dependency on all kinds of professionals who hover like vultures charging fees, mostly by the hour as this runs up the biggest bills, to provide guidance on the way through the regulatory and legal labyrinth, having ensured by helping in its creation that nobody dare enter without clutching their tacky and expensive hands. This affects the young couple starting out together scraping to buy their first home who encounter brokers, agents, surveyors and lawyers all out for their cut as much as it does great corporations whose legal bills are so huge that they make their lawyers into millionaires in the course of a single transaction.

One of the most alarming examples of where this leads is that having come up with the taxpayers' cash to bail out reckless banks, the government then had to pay these same institutions fees to advise on the implementation of their own rescue. The idea that this is somehow making money for everyone is flawed. When the music stops all the money is in China. We have all the IOUs. This is because we have built an economy that consumes more than it creates. Too much effort is required to hold the existing structure together to allow any new structure to be created. If we had a sound structure in the beginning it would need much less support and we could get on with something new.

If we were not so busy following *due process* and navigating a minefield of rules we would have realised that something had gone badly wrong much sooner, but like the hesitant pedestrian relying on the green light of our illustration above, we relied on these processes to think for us and our rules to protect us.

It is no coincidence that China has not entered recession and Japan and Germany are the first to exit. All these countries make more than they consume, China by a very wide margin. We consume more than we make, as does the United States and we are both borrowing ourselves into a financial dark age. At the heart of this mess is a flawed belief that we can prosper if other countries make things and we make money. At the heart of that is a misunderstanding of what money is, which I have already touched on, and the difference between value and worth, which I now raise for the first time.

Money is a measure. It has to be related to something to acquire worth, just as inches are useless on their own as they require something to measure to acquire purpose. A case full of cash on a desert island with nothing to buy and no prospect of transfer to a place where it can acquire worth is useless as are the late discovered notes of a defunct currency like confederate dollars. To establish money we need to use it to measure value whether it is the value of labour, knowledge, skill, talent, assets or commodities.

We saw in the inflationary binge of the late sixties and most of the seventies that if you keep increasing the money value of the same job producing the same output, all that happens is you pay out more and more yet the money buys less and less, so not only are you no better off, but many on less flexible incomes are worse off. This is why controlling inflation is a common priority of economic policy.

Having dealt with that recurrent problem in the late nineties we failed to spot that the same rule applied to assets. If you keep increasing the money value of the same assets, the worth of the asset remains constant but the value of the money diminishes. Simply put inflation and deflation equal each other as two halves of the same coin. Inflation of unimproved assets means deflation of money value and inflation of money value means deflation of assets.

 The objective should be a perfect balance, but since this is theoretically attractive but impossible in practice, a very low level of inflation is more manageable than the equivalent deflation. It must be understood that this must be achieved with as much balance as possible between one part and another and neither assets nor pay can run out ahead of the other without the whole model becoming unstable.

At the moment we are worried about deflation with things costing less and less as this leads to pay cuts and houses being worth less than we paid for them with loans which get bigger. Of course if we are sitting on a pile of cash we would welcome deflation as this makes our money buy more.

The mistake we made which all but bust the whole economy was to suppose that you could keep inflation at very low levels across the economy, except for housing which could spiral out of control up and up with no ill effect. This meant that the money being used to buy houses had a different value to the money used to buy groceries, creating a shortage causing people to borrow more and more, which to make matters worse was used to buy goods made overseas. The instability in the process eventually sucked the money out of the system and we ran out. We called it the credit crunch. In fact it was exactly the same mechanism which operated with jobs which finally blew up in the early eighties. Wages went up and up without any improvement in output until the jobs disappeared and we had three million on the dole.

Now we are creating new money in the hope of putting things right, but we know that this can, if it goes wrong, lead to absolute collapse of the currency as it did in Germany between the wars and in Zimbabwe quite recently. To avoid these worries we need to stabilise asset values so that their worth has to improve to increase their value and organise financial policy to that objective.

This will never be achieved by regulation. What is needed is a sounder financial structure upon which bedrock our economy can be rebuilt based on sound values, sound money and sound banks. The mass of the people will then to be able to go about their daily lives, building their careers, families and businesses, with a greater degree of security than there is at present. The entrepreneurs and the pioneers will then be able to push the frontiers of the market forward, always followed by a ragbag of spivs and speculators, knowing that reward beckons, but with ruin as her handmaiden.

It is the prospect of ruin which provides the best regulation. Ruin must not be allowed to become a pandemic which engulfs the innocent who never had access to the reward and so some degree of control is essential, but the sounder the structure, the less this will need to be.

50

At the heart of a well organised state is its approach to the environment. This impinges every aspect of every person's life. To that we need now to add climate change, which is often the first thought when the word environment is mentioned.

It is important to recognise that the climate of the earth is unstable and has been subject to continuous change over the ages. We all know about ice ages and advancing and retreating glaciers which literally shaped our countryside. There is evidence that once they get going these changes move quite rapidly and as they do they affect the nature and shape of life. There is also evidence that from time to time these changes are sudden and catastrophic. One may well have been the cause of the sudden extinction of the dinosaurs after dominating the earth for millions of years. The big question today is whether another such catastrophe is in prospect and whether it will be our fault.

Science is now almost united in believing that the way we live and go about our business is contributing to global warming and if we do not act, trouble, big trouble is in store. The three main sources of environmental damage are transport, heavy industry and power generation. Deforestation is an issue in some parts of the world and might have been an issue here in Iron Age times, but our problem in our country today is pollution. Following the de-industrialisation of the eighties industrial pollution is not for us quite the issue it might have been. Pollution from power generation can be resolved by scientifically capturing the harmful discharge from coal stations, from wind, hydro and solar power and of course from nuclear power stations.

The latter worry many people but I have always been comfortable and for twenty years could see one of the biggest from my bedroom window. I had not quite realised until I walked past and saw the venting stream that such power stations are just steam turbines with a different way of heating the water. Nuclear reaction is the energy which drives the universe upon which all life depends and as nature has learned to manage the risks, so should we, just as way back we learned to live with and use fire.

The big, emotive, issue is transport. Emotions rise highest whenever cars are discussed. Many see themselves through the image of their car, which they regard as a potent symbol of personal freedom. This barrier goes up whenever an attempt is made to curb the use of private cars. To put all this into perspective we need to go back to earlier times.

Transport was the source of our industrial revolution. In an island heavy loads could be carried round the coast in small ships and an amazing network of canals traversed inland to provide access to important centres. We relied less on roads which became difficult for horse drawn traffic in winter, but gradually these were given better surfaces by landowners who charged tolls for their use. Along came the railways and changed civilisation. Not only could goods be moved in huge quantities and with ease but people had the freedom to travel as never before. It was possible at the end of the nineteenth century to step out of one's cottage in a remote village, walk a mile or two to the station, board a train and after a few changes end one's journey on the platform of some far away place of dreams like Istanbul or Venice.

The Romans built their Empire on foot, but we built ours by sea and by rail. Not always was the use helpful. The Germans found railways were good for moving armies and built their network with that in mind. Abraham Lincoln was a railway lawyer and helped to provide his state of Illinois with the highest railway concentration in the world. It was the greater railway network of the north that helped to defeat the less well integrated system of the south, giving the Yankees an advantage in speedy transportation of troops and supplies. The lesson was well learned in Europe.

Here in our island we had invented the whole thing and were the pioneers. It was possible to go almost anywhere by rail, though the smaller lines followed a less direct route and lacked the glamour, sparkle and comfort of the crack expresses on the main lines. Civilised life, not to mention industry, commerce and businesses of all kinds were so integrated into the railway network that life without it was no longer possible to imagine. There was, anyway no alternative.

Until the advent of the car, the spluttering early days of which, spent coughing along slowly behind a man carrying a red flag, did not at once foretell the world dominance to which it would one day rise, not just as transport, but as industry, icon, image and love, all combined. As the car advanced upon its beguiling journey, we began to use it more and neglect the railways until we let them go to pot. Annoyed by the cost of unpunctual, smutty and now nationalised trains, the government responded by calling in an expert, not in railways but in business, and took his recommendation to close a third of the network. This made travel by car a necessity rather than a treat.

Never mind, because now motor car manufacture of which we were one of the world's biggest and certainly the best, had become our most important industry. Other countries were busy modernising their railways and their motor industry. We all know the sorry end of the tale. We ended with sub standard railway starved of investment and no home owned motor industry at all. The Japanese and the Germans came to the rescue of our car industry, more recently followed by the Indians, whose industrial magnates have management skills of large workforces that our own apparently lacked.

The French set us up with a start at railway improvement with the high speed line from London to Paris. There is talk of more high speed lines but there is no rural network any longer. Meanwhile we hardly care because we love our cars so much.

That has to change. Either face the fact that the day of the car is over, or face the prospect that our days may be over too. If we get on with this now it will cause a lot less pain later. We have to alter our perception of motoring. It is a convenience, sometimes a liberating opportunity to get about and it can be fun, but it is not freedom. We have to use our cars less and use less polluting cars when we do. Already there are signs that people are buying smaller cars. This helps but we have to do something more than that. As I am not a politician, I can say it. Electronic road pricing is the best and fairest option.

It can be very flexible. Country dwellers would have so many free miles per month to make up for a lack of public transport and this would help people on low incomes. Those on benefits of various kinds could have free miles, all by coding the sensor in their car. Town dwellers would not have free miles because of access to public transport. Petrol taxes would be reduced and road tax abolished. Public transport subsidies would reduce because of wider use. Some routes would be more costly than others to reduce congestion, but the objective would be to increase the cost of unnecessary journeys by car.

Of course it would help if good schools were in every community to cut out the school run and if hospitals and health centres were near where their patients lived. This is the opposite of the short sighted, economy driven, policy of successive governments over many years; a disaster which

323

will take a long time to clear up. Every public policy will have to be directed to cutting journey length, from engineers being based miles from their customer call out area to weekend doctors covering half a county. Note how cosy these same politicians kept their own work environment. We do not see Whitehall in Manchester and Downing Street in Southampton.

The more carbon neutral cars can be made the more we shall be able to use them and government has some responsibility to encourage and fund research and apprenticeships to speed the process. The commercial gains for successful designs are almost endless, so the industry itself can be relied upon to make quite an effort, but this is the most pressing of modern challenges and every resource must be applied.

Because of the decline of our railway network almost all goods now travel by road. This is a bad thing from many angles and from the environmental angle very bad indeed. There is no public transport alternative now available for freight and lorries will be harder to make carbon neutral than small cars. Something can be done to source near manufacture and make near market, but that will not be practical in many cases nor enough where it is possible. We need to modernise our railway network.

As we discovered nearly two centuries ago more weight can be transported with less energy by rail than any other land transport. Now we are able to do this without dangerous carbon emissions. We must develop a network of high speed lines and reintroduce freight on the slower lines. This will mean new goods yards and other infrastructure but we really have no choice. We should also re-lay as many as possible of our branch lines to become rural tramways. We must restore our transport network to its efficiency and coverage of a century ago. It would make a major impact on our carbon footprint and create real new jobs both in reconstruction and subsequent operation. It would then create the leeway for us to use low carbon cars less out of necessity of work and more for fun in leisure.

Eventually circumstances will force action upon us. To avoid this being hasty and dramatic we need to make a start soon. Patching what remains of our Victorian transport heritage is no longer sufficient. It will be expensive, though private enterprise will have many opportunities for profit. Shutting down the Quango State and reducing the size of government will free up resources to make a start.

51

This book has been mainly about England, because with devolution, much in government that we have discussed is devolved to Scotland, Wales and Northern Ireland. This has been of great benefit to all three countries and I am an enthusiastic supporter. I am entirely relaxed if all three held referenda and voted to become independent. This is generally unlikely, except for Scotland.

Scotland really is a separate country. Never occupied either by the Romans or the Normans it has a proud and different heritage and has contributed much to the richness of Great Britain, as part of which its people have been at the vanguard of some of our greatest achievements. It has its own legal system which is quite different to ours and its own education system, renowned throughout the world. Its legal system has been brought into sharp focus worldwide as I write this, because of the decision to release the Lockerbie Bomber, as Ali al-Megrahi has come to be known.

Before I give my views, I want to share a thought about the pain felt by those brave relatives left with lifelong grief through the loss of their loved ones on that ill fated plane. I know the hurt of such grief as I too have lost, in different circumstances the only common feature being that my child's death need not have happened. I know too that the hurt does not diminish with time, as people tell you it will to bring you comfort, if anything it gets worse. You are left in permanent shock forever haunted by that day, that hour, that moment. That moment which carves your life into two parts; before and after.

The only course before you, strewn with poignant memories which bring joy and tears in equal measure, is to learn to live a life from which the impact of that terrible loss will never be smoothed away. Strength comes from the care and warmth of friends and family and in the case of a disaster, from those who share your experience. You can gain strength from seeing justice served, but here there is a warning. If the wish for justice becomes a thirst for revenge, no comfort will be found. Vengeance sears the scars yet deeper. Mercy is a tonic which will do much to heal, but only forgiveness, the highest aspiration of humanity and the hardest of all to reach, will bring peace.

To know what, why and by whom is a necessary part of the process, for without, one cannot know who or what is to blame or where to mend or punish or forgive. This is where a problem may well arise. There are some crimes which are

327

so complex that their solution by ordinary means within the lifespan of those affected may prove impossible. This is because they are the work of many hands, odd alliances and conflicting interests. If a culprit is run to earth, fair trial may be impossible, because so many others have melted away, so much evidence has been withheld and other evidence tampered with to provide false trails, that is impossible to know if one is judging a fiend or a fall guy.

We can look at some enduring mysteries. The shooting down of the Iranian airliner by the USS *Vincennes* of the U.S Navy is a good place to start, on July 3 1988, as it happened just six months before Lockerbie. The plane was entirely a civilian airliner, flying in its own airspace, carrying sixty six children together with adult passengers and crew making a total compliment of two hundred and ninety. All perished when the plane was deliberately shot down by a missile fired from this U.S warship, which explained the calamity on its inability to distinguish between an attacking fighter jet and a passing passenger plane.

This explanation is clearly absurd, unless we are to assume naval incompetence without parallel. The United States refused to admit blame and awarded medals to the crew. It only paid compensation for the loss of the plane and to the families of the victims seven years later after being taken to the International Court of Justice by Iran. The figures are interesting. The U.S paid a total of $181 million. This compares with the $ 2.8 billion offered by Libya, with strings attached, for Lockerbie. Not all these strings were met but $8 million per family of the victims was paid in the U.S., although some neither sought compensation nor took it. The extraordinary difference in value of human life between one nationality and another, one must suppose, reflect differences in economic conditions in each country. Nevertheless it is a discomforting comparison.

Many people believe, I am persuaded they may be right, that the blowing up of the Pan Am 103 was connected to the shooting down of Iran Air 655. What is clear is that it was not the work of a single fanatic working alone. This is the same question which haunts other mysteries, even after enquiries appear to close the matter. Was the Titanic disaster just down to Captain Smith? Did Hess all of a sudden go mad and jump in a plane and fly to Scotland on a whim? Was Oswald a lone fanatic who shot Kennedy as the many volumes of the Warren Commission conclude? Was Diana and Dodi's driver really that drunk and they did not notice?

Sometimes disasters are so sudden that it is difficult to unravel for certain the sequence of events. Sometimes accidents are so peculiar they defy explanation. Sometimes crimes are so big and involve so many that they cannot be resolved by normal judicial process. Lockerbie is like that. I call them State Crimes, where trying one participant is no more than symbolic. Unfortunately such trials never can conform to the definition of a fair trial, because too many agencies have a hand in determining what evidence shall be seen and what is withheld. Scotland made an heroic effort to be fair after Lockerbie so that justice would be seen to be done and convicted one of the accused and released another.

But it was not a normal trial. It took place in Holland, a piece of which was deemed to be Scotland for the purpose, without a jury, the normal guarantee of fair play. The three judges did their utmost but in the end their judgement could only be as good as the evidence put before them. It now turns out that this was not complete. For years wise and distinguished public and legal figures have campaigned that al-Megrahi is not the man. He certainly cannot have been the only one.

That this was a state sponsored attack cannot be in doubt; which State or what combination working together less so. The solution cannot lie in arraigning a single official of one potentially guilty country. This is not fair, nor is it justice nor does it provide solution. We have to find a quite different format of enquiry and retribution for high crimes committed by states against the innocent victims of the other, where some form of tribunal makes public what is known even if this falls short of a conclusion. This level of crime cannot possibly be properly resolved by the same process as fits a robbery or a conventional murder, because whoever pulls the trigger, plants the bomb or blows themselves and everybody else up is just the smallest cog in a much more dangerous and very much larger wheel. The biggest mistake we have made about terrorists is to treat them as common criminals, when they are disciplined quasi-military conglomerations who regard us, even our innocent little children, as mortal enemies.

The decision by the Scottish Justice Secretary to release the Lockerbie bomber was taken on compassionate grounds according to the tenets of Scottish, not American nor English, law. It is the kind of decision the responsibility for which few would volunteer. The volume of interventions and lobbying beforehand was at maximum, yet in a very moving address the Minister showed that his duty to show Mercy according to his country's legal system was the driver which made up his mind.

Some may argue that showing mercy to terrorists encourages more to come forward. This is not so. Modern terrorists give their lives with pride and have no mercy for their victims. Treating like with like results in stalemate. Showing compassion and mercy in the right circumstances just might cause a potential recruit to the jihad cause to stop and wonder. What is needed is a propaganda impact to stem the recruitment zeal. Anyone who argues that the fear of prison if caught will deter potential terrorists has just not been paying attention. Our judgements must be based on our values, our civilisation, our faith and our ideals. These must shine brighter than those which challenge them.

In showing mercy to this dying man, however heinous the crime for which he had been convicted but may not have been solely or even guilty, Scotland led the world in showing that the only route to healing is to offer compassion according to the best traditions of almost every peaceful faith by rising above the wickedness which snatched all those innocent lives. In doing so the minister brought out the best in himself and all those who counselled him upon his course. He also brought out the worst in almost everyone else.

The way in which many politicians have been scoring points by asserting the nonsense that some vengeful lust will be satisfied if this wretched sufferer from cancer expires in his cell, has demeaned us all. In contrast the restraint and compassion of many, though not all, of the relatives has been remarkable.

The intervention of American officials in their bullying assault on the bewildered Scottish Government was symptomatic of anger in their country. It was also wrong, but in this dreadful episode lie certain lessons for our own country too. Never must justice be confused with revenge, never shall we become so debased we cannot forgive and to punish you must first discover the full truth of the crime.

We can remind ourselves that we brought reconciliation to terrorist insurgencies in Cyprus, Kenya and Northern Ireland. In the former two we built warm relations with governments on whose leader's heads we had once laid a price. In Northern Ireland to aid reconciliation we have released from prison many responsible for the atrocities committed during the IRA campaign which killed over six hundred civilians, sixty in England. It would have been good if the United States had paused, curbed its anger and realised that in our ways lie some very useful lessons.

52

One of the elements of modern government is the Public Enquiry. Another is the Review. They are used in different ways. Let us begin with the review.

This is a symptom of bad government. It means the government knows there is a problem, but has lost its way. It is not sure what to do and is keen to find out what people are thinking. When it feels on safer ground it will cherry pick the outcome and make it policy. If the issue is really sensitive and the government is on dodgy ground, it will generally accept the recommendations in full. At first sight this consultative process appears to be democratic, but it is not. The democratic process is sidelined and handed over to government appointees, however worthy. This all needs to be changed.

First of all government must keep a tighter rein on its activity. It must not undertake too much and it must keep on top of what it does. Civil servants must be given clear not muddled objectives and be held to account. Bad ones need to go. Government is supposed to be about ideas and if it runs out of them it should go too. However, if there is good reason for a review this should be decided by parliament, not government, with the review appointed by and reporting to the relevant select committee. Government could ask parliament to set up a review on an issue, but would be barred from doing so itself. A barren government needs to be exposed.

A more responsive democratic structure of the kind we have discussed earlier, would take all this in its stride. Both Houses would be filled with wider and deeper talent and governments would have a good proportion of non politicians. If things began to go off the rails the Crown would be required by statute to go back to the people. The need for reviews should be very much reduced.

Public Enquiries are altogether different. Broadly they fall into two categories. The first is some kind of disaster where the scale or circumstances make a coroner's inquest insufficient. Perhaps the most notorious of these is the Bloody Sunday Enquiry. This has at time of writing still not reported four years after completing its hearings and over ten years after it was set up. So far it has cost £181 million, of which half has gone to lawyers. The lead counsel is reported to have received £ 4 million. It begins to look like little better than a public swindle. The victims and their families, none of whom can other than dream about such

336

sums, are left waiting at the end of the queue for answers month after month, year after year, to the point where the enquiry itself has become an outrage on its own.

The second kind of enquiry is when the government itself gets into a scrape, such as the embargo on selling arms to Iraq, which led to the Scott Enquiry and the tragic death of Dr. David Kelly which led to the Hutton Enquiry. Published in 1996 Scott was thorough but allowed those he criticised to see and argue privately for softer treatment prior to publication, which process was orchestrated by the government to ensure that whilst criticised ministers were given ample time to view and prepare their defence, the opposition had just two hours to devour a million words prior to the debate on the matter in the Commons. The government won by just one vote to give itself a few more months of ineffectual rule before its electoral oblivion in 1997.

Hutton was rather different, dealing with the distressing issue of the suicide of an important civil servant following what amounted to government bullying over his anxiety about the claims that Iraq possessed weapons of mass destruction, made in the infamous dossier cooked up by the government to make its dodgy case for the invasion of Iraq.

The enquiry itself went well and earned widespread praise, but when the conclusions were published they were so at variance with what people thought the evidence indicated that there was an outcry. In fact all the blame was put on the BBC which lost talent at the top which could not readily be spared. Meanwhile the government claimed exoneration, but beyond Whitehall the whole thing fell into disrepute. A new enquiry has just been set up to look at all aspects of the Iraq war and doubtless many hope for a reliable outcome, but I have serious doubts, on evidence past, that it will prove possible to offer at the end a robust and conclusive verdict.

We need to change the nature of these enquiries. They are important and one is needed over the Lockerbie bombing, but we cannot have the vast expense and longevity of the process thus far and we must have something which is nearer the public and further from government. A Public Enquiry (Inquiry if you prefer) must be public in the widest sense. Its aim is to provide the people with all the facts hidden within the issue so as to enable them to learn what exactly did happen and the reasons why. It should not be a government enquiry open to the public. That is not enough.

The first change is to have it appointed and set up by parliament, not by the government, although the government could request it. Equally, parliament could set one up against the government's wishes. Its members would be chosen by parliament through a select committee and its Chair would be required to report regularly to the committee in public examination on progress and cost.

Next we have to establish that this is an enquiry where people speak freely and without fear and not a court. Lawyers would have no part in it, unless called to give evidence, and no legal fees could be charged either to the enquiry itself or to witnesses. Attendance of witnesses would be compulsory in law, but such witnesses would have immunity from prosecution if their evidence could be self incriminating. This may make it more difficult to punish, but these enquiries should not take place if there has been a crime with sufficient evidence to charge suspects. Their purpose is to unravel a sequence and get at the truth and this will not happen if there is anyone involved who can benefit from the truth being withheld.

In addition to experts, civil servants, or other professionals, including lawyers, there would be lay members. None would charge fees. All would receive the same allowance.

Serving would be seen as a valuable public duty. All documents would be public property and available to all. Formal conclusions would be presented where evidence allowed it but if incomplete or incapable of reliable interpretation, the enquiry could leave the conclusion open, like an open verdict in a coroner's court. These enquiries would have a statutory maximum length of a year and would be expected to report three months after completing the hearing of evidence. If this was impractical parliament alone would be able to grant extensions.

Doubtless snags would arise with this system as in the other, but these proposals would ensure a more timely and cost effective approach to finding the truth and be much closer to the public, on whose behalf and for whom it would function. It would remove from government a route of deception, concealment and whitewashing and bring to interested parties a much more vigorous and reliable route to the truth.

We need this change in order to have at our disposal leaner, keener methods of meeting the public interest when the normal processes of investigation cannot deliver. To continue with the costly quasi legal processes described by one lawyer as 'a financial godsend' is just not good enough in today's world. They take too long, have a poor record of achievement and because they are government appointed, when political issues are investigated, lack the credibility they need to carry weight into that real world beyond Westminster.

53

Too much of modern life, as I have already said, is a process and too much of that is a legal process. If a state constantly introduces new laws and regulations the burden on life and on the economy becomes excessive. Because of the weight of cost and delay this imposes, the economy become unresponsive and prone to mishap. A by-product is the ever growing need for and cost of lawyers.

Such is the size and cost of all this legal activity that it has become an economy of its own within the economy. We have seen from figures set out above for the Bloody Sunday enquiry just how much of a drain on the taxpayer and on business these fees are. This has to change. Lawyers are wonderful when they are truly needed, but if they become a component of public policy management they become a drain upon everything else. We have to cut back the legal state to free up the lay state beneath it, which struggles to breath.

This can be done several ways. The most obvious is to cut regulation and legislation so as to make every day life and business less of a legal entanglement. Another is to ban government departments and local authorities from using outside law firms. They have their own in house lawyers and if it is so complicated even they cannot cope there is something wrong.

Conveyancing of private houses should not be a legal process and there should be no lawyers or legal fees in selling or buying houses for personal occupation. Through the land registry it would not be difficult to issue every property with a certificate similar to the log book of a car. This would cause some anguish to solicitors but they have had a very good run with what is almost a bogus process designed for their exclusive benefit at everyone else's cost.

This does not mean we should not have lawyers, or that they are not good and worthy people. What is clear is that the size of their estate has grown so big that it is now all pervasive and sucking up precious resources needed elsewhere. We need to cut it down to size. The same may be said of some consultants and freelance experts of many different kinds. All have expertise which is vital and their knowledge can make all the difference. Unfortunately their excessive use by government, who should not need such people at all, has led to tens of millions of taxpayers' money being wasted, in some cases for projects which become so muddled they are abandoned.

To deal with this we need not so much reform as changes of habit and working practices. Much comes back to restoring personal responsibility, putting people in charge and judging them on the outcome. The best rise to the challenge and the worst are exposed, unable to conceal their lack of ability beneath a cloak of due process and consultative delay. The manual is no substitute for the mind. Shareholders and taxpayers must become more intolerant of senior executives and civil servants who take charge of projects which they do not understand and then waste money on consultants because of their own lack of competence for the job in hand.

One of the most frightful examples is the little reported Chinook helicopter farce. Eight Chinook helicopters were ordered from Boeing in 1995, but when delivered in 2001, unable to fly because they had no active software. This was because the British wanted to design their own, although told by Boeing that it would be unlikely to work, which in the event was the case. Now the helicopters are being modified to fly as ordinary cooking models without the combat protection necessary for battlefield service. Since 2001 all eight have been kept in a centrally heated hanger, while our troops are dying in Afghanistan, because the army is short of helicopters and has to make risky journeys by road exposed to Taliban bombs and mines.

Not only has the cost of the project doubled to £500 million, but the helicopters when they eventually fly years late will be at a much lower specification than the original plan. Meanwhile nobody knows for sure how many young soldiers are dead because of this glaring ineptitude, but it is quite a number. We simply cannot permit this kind of bungling in the management of our country in future. Sending troops into battle while their equipment languishes at home because of the feckless incompetence of those in cosy jobs with fat pensions to look forward to, is not war. It is murder.

Right across the spectrum of public management there is a catalogue of bungle, waste, more waste and confusion. Nobody is ever brought to book, held responsible or punished. When apprehended, if indeed they ever are, they no doubt wave adherence to some insane manual in their defence. In China, I read, public officials who blunder on an heroic scale can find themselves shot. Whilst not advocating quite so drastic a turn in our country, it is not difficult to see that the Chinese have a point. We cannot go on as we are for sure.

345

We must find a means to stop this prolific disregard of duty to deliver a proper outcome for public resources and when it happens ensure that those responsible have to pay a very heavy price indeed. By restoring personal responsibility and accountability by sweeping aside the protection of following due process, we shall see more clearly the heads upon which the axe should fall.

54

For our country, now approaching the end of the first decade of the twenty first century, we need a model rather different to the creaking leviathan to which we cling today. I believe it should be a new shape. It will incorporate parts previously thought be the sole province of ideology of both left and right at the same time.

Small government, local control, personal responsibility, less borrowing, more thrift, sounder money, red tape bonfires are all ideas which form part of the tradition, though not always the practice, of the right.

Public ownership of essential utilities, universal free education of the highest quality, public healthcare which delivers timely comfort and cure to patients which cannot be faulted, nationalisation of the High Street banks, restoring employment to communities, making more of what we buy, respecting the vocational as much as the academic, reducing excessive pay, these are all proposals which find favour with the left.

A refocusing of our foreign policy upon more independent lines, a single rate of income tax with all low paid lifted out of tax are ideas which we have not tried before, so they fall outside the old ideological divide.

Reconstructing our democracy on much more modern lines, giving to the people power from which they have been too long excluded, rebalancing the relationship between government and parliament and crown and people, outlawing a whole political class, comes in combination close to revolution.

The common cause of all these ideas is that they represent a practical way forward at each level of national life. How much we can do and in what order will depend on many things, beyond the scope of this narrative to explore. Our country is more in debt than at any time in its history and the scale of public borrowing both here and in the United States is now projected beyond the competence of anyone to predict with accuracy where it might lead.

The purpose of this book is to help you decide where you would like your country to go. Maybe you might like to help guide it. In the pitch of darkness, just one light has to shine.